ALL ABOUT GAZEHOUNDS

ALL ABOUT
GAZEHOUNDS

Joanna Russell

PELHAM

First published in Great Britain by
PELHAM BOOKS LTD
52 Bedford Square, London WC1B 3EF
1976

ISBN 0 7207 0926 1

Set and printed in Great Britain by
A. Wheaton & Co., Exeter

CONTENTS

To
Giggle

Introduction

For thousands of years the Gazehound has been the companion and much-prized possession of man. Even in the Islamic Culture, which considers dogs unclean, the Sighthound has been and still is regarded as a sacred animal. The worship of these hounds can be simply explained by the extraordinary beauty of a Greyhound at full stretch, the flashing feathered limbs of the Saluki on the desert wastes and the slow-motion stride of the Deerhound on the rough terrain of Scotland. The exhilarating experience of watching a long dog in action, combined with the practical knowledge of his ability to provide essential sustenance for the nomadic families of the Middle East, do much to account for the immense admiration and respect historically and at present accorded to him.

For the sentimental, the expression in the eye and the exquisite attitude in repose are reward enough, but for the lover of sport there is nothing more enjoyable than to walk over stubble on a frosty morning and watch two dogs put up a tremendous demonstration of speed, cunning and stamina while pitting their wits against another living animal. For the gambler, the flashing circuit of the race track under the arc lights provides intense excitement and, for the aesthetic eye, the clean, flowing lines of a running hound give unique pleasure.

In short, Gazehounds are probably the most versatile of any canine group and have been used to provide sport and entertainment for their owners since they were first bred in the Middle East. Since then they have been developed, worked and prized in every country of the world.

Before people wrote or made pictures that have survived, what was the history of the dog in England? When did it first come to our islands? The dog is descended from the wolf and the wolf probably existed before the Ice Age and was still extant in Scotland until 1743.

9

The early wolf mated with the fox and the jackal and a variety of animals resulted, which changed in conformation as a result both of habitat and the quarry available. During the glacial period a number of tamed wolves and dogs were almost certainly kept by Palaeolithic Man (whether River Drift Man, Neanderthals or Cro-Magnons) for guard duties, companionship, food and entertainment.* 'The glaciations (there were more than one) didn't actually invade Southern England' and it is reasonable to assume that the same strange men in our land whom Matthew Arnold describes as 'dark Iberian', or their predecessors, were as customarily and domestically involved with animals as those who dwelt in the caves of Lascaux. Here drawings of animals are brilliantly executed on the rock face and date from 30,000 *BC,* and in the Altamira caves in Spain there are others from 15,000 *BC.*

Because the climate was tropical in northern Europe before the last Ice Age, and the whole northern landmass abounded with large game, unquestionably wolves and dog types existed in 30,000 *BC.* Subsequently, pockets of Palaeolithic men and probably dogs remained here on the edge of the ice cap until its retreat in 10,000 *BC* and the emergence of the true *Homo sapiens* in northern Europe.

At this distant time Britain was joined to the Continent — southward into France and eastward into Germany. The confluent Rhine and Thames merged and split into a north-eastern sea. Even after the melting ice cap swamped the land bridge, during the Mesolithic and early Neolithic era of about 6,000 - 8,000 *BC,* low tide provided shallows. It was across here that man and his dog must have moved to and fro. When Kent and Picardy lost their link the traveller used a skin boat.** 'Ghost men who flit in the mists of long ago' is a useful description of Palaeolithic and Neolithic men and is splendidly suggestive of both man and beast.

The early history of England is a history of invasions and of forest life. Due to an environment of dense forest, the dogs that Neolithic men brought over were probably Huskies. Fernand Mery, in his book *The Dog,* opens most interestingly

* J. A. Williamson, *The English Channel.*
** G. M. Trevelyan, *History of England.*

on this subject. He also quotes Scandanavia as having the greatest number of remains of domestic dogs in Europe, dating from before 7,000 *BC*.

Mery picks out three primitive breeds that are Neolithic coevals, one of which is the Greyhound. This he believes to have come from Africa and the Near East. Now, despite the thick undulating expanses of forest in England, there were undoubtedly clearings; there were portions of downland and there were coastal strips. All the open spaces were suitable for Gazehounds to work. Cornish minerals attracted trade and with the traders came their animals. This commerce was particularly active between the Mediterranean and south-western England. English jet, dating from 2,500 *BC*, has been found in Spain. The Bronze Age men of 2,000 *BC* were apparently avid exchangers and traders.

So it is reasonable to assume that with this trade in minerals there was also a trade in animals. Undoubtedly this was the origin of the first Gazehounds in England.* 'The area of origin of the ideas, if not of all people's constituting the neolithic movement, was in the Middle East where the use of domestic animals is traceable at much earlier periods than in the North West.' From earliest Neolithic times the Greyhound type had existed in North Africa, as shown by the rock drawings of the Tassili Mountains in Algeria and southern Libya.

Once the forests became penetrable in England and once hunting became fully dependent on the dog, the Gazehound began to fulfil an essential role in English social and economic life, as it had done for centuries in the Near East. The Bayeux tapestry is indicative of the attention devoted by the Normans to the hound group. This love of, and dependence on, the Gazehound subsequently increased and, despite the broad span of time and changing outlook that separates us from our primeval and medieval forbears, it remains just as evident today.

The customary pleasure for the Gazehound owner is to see his dog tensed and poised on the crest of a hill surveying the landscape below for moving game. This is an unfamiliar sight

* Trevelyan, *History of England.*

to the majority of sportsmen whose Retrievers or Terriers hunt nose to the ground. Not all sighthounds hunt by eye alone. Some have excellent scenting powers but, before moving in any one direction, they will always spy their quarry at the outset.

All Gazehounds originated in the Middle East and derive from the earliest Greyhound type that Mery speaks of. Nobody is certain whether the first long dogs were more akin to the Saluki, the Greyhound or the Pharaoh Hound. The latter, or dogs very similar to them, have been found in paintings on the walled tombs of the pharaohs. It is certain that a Greyhound type existed from before the earliest Dynastic times.

Unquestionably the nature of the terrain in the Middle East contributed to the habit of hunting by sight. When faced with an immense expanse of desert with sparse cover, a dog is more inclined to hunt by eye than by nose. Over a long period of time the dogs moved north and west in the wake of human migration and in the van of civilisation. In the cold mountains of Afghanistan and in the rugged freezing Caucasus their conformation, characteristics and colourings naturally altered, but the instinct and initiative of the basic stock to hunt by sight has remained unchanged after seventy centuries. Interestingly, some of the earliest artistic records of Egypt show that the dogs that the artist's eye beheld 4,000 years before Christ would not look out of place chasing a dummy hare at the White City this week.

For hundreds of years the Greyhound type existed in varying sizes from the Whippet up to the present-day Irish Wolfhound, although the Irish breed as we know it was developed much later. Plainly, one must allow for artistic licence, and the scale in many paintings and sculptures is probably incorrect. But the many records of hounds accompanied by humans demonstrate unquestionably that not all running hounds were the size of the modern Greyhound and not all had his fine coat. For example, among the remains of the buried village at Ercolano in southern Italy there is a statue of a stag being attacked by found hounds. These are small dogs of Whippet or large Italian Greyhound size. There is also later artistic proof, such as R. van der Weyden's painting 'Adoration of the Kings' at the Alte Pinathek in Munich, and the sixteenth-century Berger du Jube at Chartres Cathedral. It is quite apparent that these smaller hounds have existed for a long time. Certainly they were established as a type, if not a breed, long before the miners started crossing Greyhounds with Staffordshire Bull Terriers.

The Italian Greyhound is not included in this book because it is classified and used as a Toy breed in this country. But he has origins very close to the Whippet and his existence is admitted as one of the earliest European lapdogs. So why is the Whippet said to have been developed much later?

Italian Greyhounds are more frailer-boned and bodied than the Whippet, but can nevertheless be used for sporting purposes and still have some grain of hunting instinct left in them. In America and on the Continent, where they are included in the Gazehound group, they are still used for hunting and, occasionally, for racing. Sadly the British dogs are primarily ornamental, although a few owners take them rabbiting.

The Gazehound of the desert was useless in the jungles of southern Africa, Burma and south-east Asia. But miraculously a dog similar to the Whippet reappears in the Australian dingo. An ethnic original? Who can tell? But the Whippet, whether a forerunner of the Italian Greyhound or vice versa, can claim early origins.

Further up the scale in size, and larger than the Whippet, is the Pharaoh Hound. To the inexperienced eye he looks like a prick-eared Greyhound. Apart from the frequent Egyptian portraits, there is also an example on an Athenian vase of a dog with a hunter in the Museum of Fine Arts in Boston. This is dated 460-470 *BC* and shows a dog of unmistakable Greyhound type, with erect ears and high tail. He is larger than a Whippet but smaller than a Greyhound, which fits the Pharaoh, for this should stand approximately 24 in. tall.

The Ibizan Hound is a very close relative of the Pharaoh. He is used for rabbiting in the Balearics, but is a breed not included in this book. Their breeders claim that they do not hunt primarily by sight, but by sound and scent. Although the Pharaoh also uses his acute hearing and powerful sense of smell when hunting, he very evidently scans the landscape first and continues to do so. Ibizan enthusiasts have found that when, for example, a Greyhound is crossed with an Ibizan it detracts from the resulting puppies' hunting powers because they fail to listen so acutely and use their eyes instead.

The Deerhound has sprung obviously from the rough-coated Greyhounds depicted in numbers of paintings and illustrations, including the fifteenth-century *Treatise on Falcony and Venery* at the Bibliothèque de Chantilly and Abraham Hondius' drawing dated 1682.

Early Borzoi pictures are not available but undoubtedly there must be some in Russia. Paintings of the Afghan, too, are few and far between, probably because he developed from the Saluki who was slow to come to Europe. There is a famous painting of the Nativity by the sixteenth-century painter, Veronese, showing a Saluki watching the Virgin and Child.

From these records one can deduce that the Deerhound, Greyhound, Pharaoh, Saluki and Whippet were among the earliest of the Gazehounds, with the probable addition of the Borzoi. The Afghan is a later development of the Saluki. Few, if any, artistic records have ever been brought out of Afghanistan, but it can be reasonably supposed that the Afghan developed, as his biographer Charles Harrisson suggests after Christ.

The Irish Wolfhound, as a breed, has no age at all. Under the aegis of enterprising people, this dog was bred from residual Irish Wolfdogs and outcrossed with Great Danes and Deerhounds in the 1880s.

Gazehounds share many characteristics, apart from their hunting methods. All are very affectionate; all adopt the same postures when resting or idling. Most can adapt their hunting methods. They can be taught to flush and retrieve game as well as to course it. Some will even point and, thanks to the majority of British breeders, their basic instincts have not been bred out of them.

Finally, the intention of this book is to concentrate on the present uses and achievements of the Gazehound. So many breeds have been spoilt by exclusive breeding for the show ring. Working capabilities must eventually be lost in dogs who spend generation after generation prowling round the confines of a concrete run. There can be no improvement of any working characteristic if the opportunity to work doesn't exist. Most Gazehounds in their native habitat have coursed a hare or rabbit at some stage, so the majority will adapt to hare coursing if their natural quarry used to be a wolf or a stag.

Whippets can dispatch a hare every bit as efficiently as their larger relatives. Doubts have been expressed on this score in books on the breed, which is why it is raised here. Whippets have coursed hares for many years and they are effective killers.

It is doubtful whether any Gazehound will take to racing once it has chased live game. They should be raced first. Members of this group, who have been worked on farms then subsequently introduced to racing, show little interest in an artificial lure. The intelligent animal prefers the real thing to an electrically worked dummy.

A regrettable tendency among some racing people today is to prevent their hounds running free when exercising. A number of trainers, both professional and amateur, exercise their dogs only on the lead and on the road. This is purgatory for any active dog. More than anything, Gazehounds simply love to run, whether there is a quarry in view or not.

Gazehounds are decorative and beautiful housedogs. Mr Wentworth Day admirably expresses the entirety of the Gazehound concept:

. . . But when you walk into the resurrected graves of Chaldean kings; when you tread, by the light of a flickering candle, the stifling, hot, and dusty passages of the tombs of Egyptian Pharaohs; when you burrow at Memphis beneath the hot sands of the desert or walk with flickering ghosts in the 'Stables of Antar'; when you tread, awed, among the great pillars of Karnak, and in all these places walk in a

world which was the world long before Christ—one
thousand to five-thousand years before Christ—and find
there the pictured story of the Greyhound, then the history
of the dog suddenly takes on an enormous significance.

It is easy to ask oneself—as I did lately at Luxor—why
man for four thousand years has loved, bred, kept, and
almost deified this slender, graceful creature of light,
gentleness and action.

. . . the Greyhound is gentle, is light and graceful in
symmetry, supple and strong in action. He answers the
aesthetic needs of beauty. He answers, too, the masculine
demand for strength and speed. And in gentleness he touches
that chord of feminine necessity which, long ago, made that
now almost archaic word 'gentlepeople' a synonym for
breeding, strength of purpose, gentleness of purpose,
gentleness of manner, and success in achievement.

When we review the races of dogs, as we might review
the races of men, the Greyhound stands out pre-eminent.
Four thousand years ago he had the characteristics which
made him a gentleman among dogs, an aristocrat, a person
of breeding and beauty. He has kept them today.

1

Kennel conditions, daily routine and health

It is difficult to generalise on the care of so broad a group as the Gazehounds because they vary considerably in size and coat texture, but there are certain basic conditions vital for their good health and wellbeing so I will set these out in this chapter.

Kennelling
It is essential that all Gazehounds, particularly those with fine coats, are kept dry and out of draughts. A large, square box with high, solid sides should be provided. Preferably it should be constructed on legs to solve the draught and damp problem. To eliminate air flow beneath the raised floor the sides can be extended downwards to floor level. Obviously the measurements of such a box must depend on the size of the dog but remember that, unlike other breeds, Gazehounds prefer to extend their legs fully while sleeping. So even for the diminutive types a good size of box is necessary. Whether placed in a large or small kennel, a high-sided box with a small opening at the front provides vital protection right round the animal. In a small, unheated wooden kennel, for example, it gives double insulation and in the large brick-built variety an infra-red lamp can be placed over the box for extra heat. Failing this, it can be completely covered at the top with a lid.

Bedding
Personally I have found that the finest grade of wood wool is the most satisfactory bedding for the kennel dog. It is soft for the finer-coated breeds and provides excellent cushioning round the edge of the box so that the hound can lean back comfortably. It is also extremely warm and free from

parasites, unlike straw which is neither so soft nor so malleable. When a section is separated from the bale, undoubtedly a certain amount of wood dust comes out of the bedding, but this doesn't matter very much: once the wood wool is arranged in the box no further dust comes from it. I don't bed the dogs down on it until the dust has left the atmosphere and after it has been wiped from all surfaces and lamps. I have never had any skin, eye or ear problems with dogs from this type of bedding and can thoroughly recommend it. It is usually obtainable from large packing companies.

Obviously all my house dogs are bedded on blankets, but I find Whippet puppies in particular often chew holes in these and, while they are outside, wood wool is safer.

The run
A point to remember when designing a kennel and run is that Gazehounds are great escapists. Chain-link fencing is by far the strongest of all and cannot be easily chewed or pulled away. Even the smallest hounds, such as the Whippet, can jump formidable heights. It is advisable to face the top of the fence inwards. This makes it virtually impossible for the dogs to jump out. Alternatively, the top of the run should be covered.

Similar methods should be employed for fencing the garden and, although large quantities of wire can look unattractive, this is one of the penalties of owning active dogs. A post-and-rail fence looks smart, although expensive, but again it is necessary to attach some form of wire to it and on top of it to deter any hound who is tempted to jump. Hedges can be wired on one side only so that the wire is invisible from the inside of the garden and tall, fast-growing evergreens form a successful dog-proof barrier.

Once the fencing has been decided on, it is necessary to choose a base for the run. Personally I find concrete by far the easiest to clean, but my runs are used only for puppies or adults in season. For a dog that is permanently kennelled it is a boring, hard surface, lacking the interesting smells and variation of grass. But you may then have a quagmire of mud in the winter so this, too, has serious drawbacks. Obviously for any kennelled dog the larger the run the better. There is nothing worse than to live a life pacing up and down in a very restricted space.

Routine

No Gazehound should ever be kennelled alone. They are usually quite happy when they have company, preferably of a different sex. Most sighthound breeds have gentle, sweet temperaments, but it should never be forgotten that they are hunting hounds. Thus they can and do pack together against one weak individual — or even against one who seems to be losing a fight. For this reason I am against kennelling more than two together, and I would certainly never have three in one kennel. As with people, an odd number is frequently unsatisfactory. Two dogs gang up on a single one or simply become friendly and ignore the third one.

Whether kennelled or living in the house, all dogs should have a regular routine. They should be fed at the same times and, if possible, exercised and groomed at set times too. Any animal feels secure if he knows exactly what to expect from his owner and, as for horses or humans, the biological clock is all important for health and happiness.

Feeding

Because of their streamlined conformation and tremendous energy, Gazehounds should be fed twice a day. They gallop faster and further than other breeds while out exercising, thus burning more energy and they do need to be fed after strenuous exercise. Obviously one allows a period of rest first but, once rested, they are hungry.

Basically, a dog's diet should contain balanced quantities of meat, fish, bones or bone meal, cereals, liver, milk, eggs and yeast. Given correct amounts of these, a hound should not need vitamin supplements. If a supplement is given to boost calcium intake, for example, it is vital that strict attention is given to the directions supplied with the powder or tablets. Too much can be almost as harmful as the original deficiency.

Hounds do best on raw, red meat, with fish once or twice a week. It is surprising how many kennels and pet owners feed the same tinned, dried or even fresh meat all the time to their animals. It is as boring for a dog as for his owner to have an identical diet every day. Food should be varied and it is a good idea to cook meat occasionally in a hot pot with vegetables. These can be given mixed in a stew to the dogs. Garlic is excellent for the lungs and can be cooked in with the stew or given in tablet form. Too much red meat can over-heat the blood, which is why it is important to vary the diet.

Biscuit is nearly always included in all hound meals, but an excellent alternative is baked brown bread. The cereal-flake types of meal are also good and contain oil, which helps to produce a healthy coat.

One fact about sighthounds not generally realised is that, despite their slim appearance, they eat a tremendous amount. Even a Whippet will demolish ¾ - 1 lb of meat a day and look really poor if he has less. These hounds are therefore expensive to feed and breeders should be scrupulously careful to instruct novice owners to this effect.

Feeding must be carefully regulated and no hound should be allowed to gallop on a full, heavy stomach. The best feeding times are early in the morning and between 5 and 6pm in the evening.

Exercise

No Gazehound is healthy physically or mentally without proper exercise. Lack of it can cause acute boredom and then irritability or a tendency to become destructive.

Ideally, they should be walked on the lead about one to two hours after their first feed. Two miles is an adequate distance for the smaller breeds, but the larger hounds can do with double that distance. It is also necessary to give them free galloping at some stage during the day after their road walk. A gallop for miles is fun but not absolutely vital, but free exercise in a large field or paddock is an absolute necessity. The greatest joy for a hound is that of running in plenty of space. It is positively cruel to restrict him.

So the most important facts to remember about the daily

management of sighthounds is to keep them warm, comfortable and with a companion, to exercise them regularly both on and off the lead, and to feed them according to their capacity — which is considerable.

HEALTH AND COMMON AILMENTS

The most important single piece of advice that I can give here is to consult your veterinary surgeon immediately if your dog appears less lively than normal and has ceased to eat for no apparent reason. There is nothing more tiresome for any veterinary practice than to be presented with a dog who has been getting progressively worse over a period of several days. Remember the normal temperature for a dog is 101.5°F. and a rise in temperature, when not the result of violent exercise, is usually an indication of infection. Veterinary advice should be sought at once on these occasions.

Gazehounds are very tough physically, despite their fine conformation. Most of them do feel the cold more than other breeds and tend, in old age, to suffer from kidney problems. Probably because they are so wholehearted in their exercise, they can also be affected by heart trouble, but again this does not happen usually until they are more than ten years old unless the animal has been overstrained. As they grow older, they restrict themselves naturally and have a sixth sense which tells them how much exercise they can reasonably take. But it is vital not to allow more than a brief gallop when they are less than a year old. When young, steady moderate exercise is required — not excessive speed tests.

The minor ailments that can be treated at home are as follows:

Digestive disturbances
As already stated, any dog that goes off its food for no apparent reason should be watched very carefully unless it has habitual minor stomach upsets. The fine-coated hounds often suffer from stomach chills which cause loss of appetite for about half a day. A teaspoon of brandy, mixed with a

pinch of brown sugar, is quite effective in curing this if it is administered three times a day. The dog should obviously be kept warm with either direct heat or a covered hot-water bottle in his basket.

Diarrhoea must always be treated if it persists for longer than a day. In young puppies it can occur with a change of diet, particularly after weaning. Occasionally they develop an allergy to cow's milk. Unless the puppy is obviously ill, it is merely advisable to alter its feeding until it returns to normal. When adult, however, unless it has had a drastic change of meat or biscuits, the dog should be kept under close supervision. It is sensible to have a mild, chalky, gastric mixture in the medicine cupboard (this can be obtained from your vet). This can be administered in the first day of any attack. If it fails to work, the dog probably has an infection or some type of abnormality and professional advice should be sought.

Persistent vomiting, which is frequently accompanied by a tremendous thirst, should be treated by a veterinary surgeon at once. The dog may become dehydrated very quickly in this condition. Glucose and water can be spooned into the animal's mouth in small but frequent amounts as this will help to keep his strength up and may maintain liquid in the kidneys.

Accidents
Road accidents frequently result in broken limbs. In such a case, make a splint from two pieces of wood placed either side of the leg, and bind them on with a bandage over cotton wool until veterinary help arrives. For cut arteries bind a well-padded bandage tightly all down the leg rather than use a tourniquet. If the bleeding does not stop, apply a tourniquet from a strip of material or bandage. Tie it round the wound as tightly as possible, but the pressure must be released after about twenty minutes. The best treatment for shock is to keep the animal as quiet and comfortable as possible and, above all, warm.

When coursing, racing, showing or simply driving any-where, it is sensible to carry a first-aid kit with you containing bandages, cotton wool, Dettol and healing ointment. The yellow lotion, Riboflavine, is extremely effective for healing nasty, open wounds.

Stings
The really dangerous type of sting is that caused by swallowing a wasp or a bee. The tongue then swells and the dog can choke unless prompt action is taken. It is a good idea to have a supply of antihistamine tablets and cream available, as this reduces the swelling to the minimum if administered immediately. The application of TCP or a cut onion to the sting has also proved effective.

Sprains and knocked-up toes
Both these conditions are very common in the running dog and the best cure for both is rest. With a sprain, cold compresses should be administered every few hours and the affected limb should be wrapped in an elastic bandage. The injured leg will swell and feel very hot and care should be taken to keep the dog as immobile as possible so that no weight is put on the injured limb. Knocked-up toes should also be treated with respect, otherwise they can cause long-term lameness. The toe joint is displaced so that the toe stands up at an unnatural angle.

Gentle massage with oil is very effective and the animal should be exercised on a lead only, until he is sound. This can take up to about three months. In minor cases the toe will return to normal, although it may remain a little enlarged. In more severe examples the toe may have to be removed if the dog is to gallop normally again.

Parasites
There is now an excellent shampoo available from most veterinary surgeons, which combats all parasites in the coat. It is called Alugan and is rubbed into the damp coat but should not be rinsed off. The dog should be allowed to dry naturally if possible. Ticks are the only parasites which are more difficult to eliminate. Use a pair of tweezers but take care that the head has been removed as well as the pincers.

Skin conditions

These are so varied and can have so many causes that it is not really possible to outline them all here. Any major skin condition which seems to spread quickly, causing intense irritation and loss of hair, needs prompt attention. The affected dog should be isolated in case he is afflicted by an infectious disease such as mange or ringworm. Your veterinary surgeon can take a skin scraping from the dog for testing so that the condition can be identified.

Mild skin irritations can be caused by too rich a diet or a change of bedding. Allergies can also cause lumps, redness, loss of hair, soreness or itching. So many factors can produce allergies: the washing powder used for dog blankets or coats, carpet dyes, fly and crop sprays — and these are just a few of them.

I have outlined the most likely problems you will have with your dogs, but it should be remembered that all puppies should be immunised against the major canine diseases at about twelve weeks. These are: distemper, hardpad, hepatitis and leptospirosis. The injections are normally given in two doses, two weeks apart, and the dog should have a yearly booster thereafter. The vaccines are extremely effective, but outbreaks of disease can and do occur, particularly in areas where there are numbers of strays, so it is vital that one's dogs should be protected against them.

2

Breeding

We can now consider the basic necessities for breeding a healthy and otherwise successful litter.

There are several golden rules to be remembered and put into practice. The first is that no matter how careful you may be in your choice of stud dog and the care of your bitch, you may still breed an indifferent litter. On the other hand, you may achieve instant success. One certainty is that you have far more chance of producing a good litter of puppies if you take care and trouble over the whole process, rather than simply use the most convenient dog on an indifferent bitch.

No litter should be bred without good reason. The prime reasons for bringing puppies into the world are:

1. To continue a well-proved bitch line, in which case one would be keeping a puppy oneself.
2. To placate a bitch plainly frustrated by the fact that she has no puppies. In this type of case I am not referring to the subject of false pregnancies — which constitute quite another problem — but to the bitch determined to foster a kitten, a puppy not her own etc. This is undoubtedly a sign of frustrated motherhood, but it doesn't occur often.
3. If an entire litter of puppies is booked by known and tested homes.
4. If your bitch is outstanding in any field, it is arguable that, with the potential she undoubtedly possesses, she should be bred from. Good homes for the progeny of such an animal are more easily found and the owner can afford to pick and choose the most reliable owners from those available.

There can be no other valid reason for breeding a litter, apart from those mentioned above. I would like to explode

25

once and for all the popular theory that no bitch is complete without having produced at least one litter. There is absolutely no reason whatsoever why any bitch should produce puppies, and this applies particularly to pet bitches. There are far too many dogs in Britain today. Nearly all breeds have a rescue scheme and all these are bursting at the seams with unwanted dogs needing homes. It is irresponsible to breed puppies unless their future is assured. Gazehounds, in any case, are most unsuited to the restricted lives so many people are forced to live today. Unless they are offered a life with the sort of freedom they enjoy, it is not only pointless, but also unkind, to breed them.

Choice of stud dog
Having established that one has a valid reason for breeding in the first instance, one's second consideration must be the choice of a stud dog. Obviously one's first bitch is all important so it is taken for granted that she is a good specimen of the breed with a kind temperament. In choosing a male for her it is necessary to decide whether one is looking for speed, stamina, looks, type or, ideally, a dog which combines all four qualities. For the novice — and obviously this chapter is not written for the experienced — it is wise to study the progeny of the dog you select. Remember like does not necessarily beget like and an outstanding, well-constructed dog may not produce progeny up to his own standard. It is wise, therefore, to choose an animal who has served a number of bitches. It is far from sensible to judge a dog on one litter. If it is a superb one, the bitch may have had a great influence on the progeny. If his first litter is unpromising, the bitch may have been indifferent or her bloodlines may not have suited those of the sire.

The other important point to remember is type. Presumably you will have chosen a bitch that was the type you wanted to breed, so choose a dog of similar stamp and make sure that on paper the bloodlines of the two dogs go well together. Line breeding is not in-breeding and if you choose a dog with *similar* breeding to your bitch you then have a chance of producing the type you want. Study the pedigree of both dog and bitch and discover as much as you can about their ancestors. Usually you will find several who have had a great influence on their descendants and it is wise to keep to the lines of the influential dogs you particularly admire.

Obviously, with beginner's luck, one may well breed a superb litter from a complete outcross and without studying pedigrees at all, but for the benefit of future generations bred from your stock, it is far wiser to start the right way. Disappointing results from an outcross can occur in future generations.

Colour

One other factor to consider is that breeding for colour can lead you to despair. Fawn and brindle are both dominant colours, but if you depend on a litter of either of these colours it is wise to try to choose a sire and dam who are fawn or brindle-bred for several generations. Particolours and whites have a habit of appearing for no apparent reason, even when parents and grandparents are solid colours.

Breeding for blacks and blues is yet another matter and only a colour specialist with many years experience of breeding for colour can give an indication of what to expect from a mating of coloured parents. Two blacks don't necessarily make a litter of blacks, as this colour is recessive. Depending on the ancestry of the parents, the combination can even make a litter of whites! Blue is more predictable in that with one blue parent there is usually at least one blue puppy in the litter.

Care of the bitch in whelp

Having chosen the best bitch available in the first place, and having mated her to the best dog you can find, you then wait to see if the bitch is in whelp. Early on, the only signs you are likely to detect are slightly enlarged teats or perhaps a change in her appetite. Some bitches experience slight sickness. Others develop a ravenous appetite, although this usually occurs a little later on. At five weeks one ought to be able to see a slight thickening round the loin. As this increases there can be no doubt of her condition and she should then gradually be given extra food. Three meals a day should be given rather than two. If her normal diet is about ¾lb of meat a day it is stepped up to 1lb, then 1½lb per day.

Hounds tend to bump each other while exercising and push together when going through doors and gates. The pregnant bitch must be protected from this for her puppies could be injured. No violent exercise, such as leaping gates or flat-out galloping, should be allowed over the last few weeks.

During the last ten days her whelping box should be prepared. This can either be the completely enclosed variety, inside which the body temperature of both the bitch and puppies should remain at the correct level, or the type of box I have described in the kennelling chapter. Bitch and puppies must be kept very warm, but they mustn't be allowed to get too hot as this will make the bitch uncomfortable and possibly irritable. About 70°F. is the right temperature and if the mother is relaxed and obviously comfortable, with the puppies quiet and content, then plainly the conditions surrounding them are correct. There must be space in an open-topped box for the mother and puppies to move away from the direct beam of the lamp if they so wish. No lamp should be so low over the box that the bitch knocks against it as she moves around. It is also unwise to have easily accessible wires coming from it.

A few days before the bitch is due to whelp, start feeding her in the kennel where she will produce the puppies so that she becomes accustomed to the surroundings. But if she is a housedog, don't leave her in there until she starts to whelp — she may panic in an unfamiliar place.

Whelping
Detailed information on this subject can be obtained from the many books devoted entirely to breeding and written by specialists. Gazehounds are easy whelpers, but problems do occur when, for example, the bitch is carrying just one very large puppy, or if a dead puppy is present. Obviously the bitch should be watched very carefully for the day following the whelping in case she still has an unborn puppy or afterbirth inside her. This occurs rarely, however. When the

bitch shows obvious signs of whelping she will want her owner with her, particularly if it is her first litter. If she is very restless and upset between producing her puppies, remove those that have been born into a dry cardboard box, with a covered hot-water bottle, until she has produced the next arrival. Normally the bitch will clean the puppies and sever the umbilical cord herself, so there is no need for her owner to interfere. At the outset the animal may need soothing if she is very frightened. Usually about three puppies are produced, then the bitch has a rest of an hour or more before the next one is born. However, if the gap between puppies is prolonged and the bitch is straining and in distress without any sign of a puppy coming, it is wise to consult your veterinary surgeon.

After-care

After the puppies are born the bitch will not want to leave them for more than a few minutes to eat or to go outside. She should be fed on white meat or fish for the first three days after the whelping, then gradually put back on to meat again. Obviously while she is feeding a litter her food intake should be doubled at least and she should be fed four or five times a day, with constant access to milk and water. When the puppies are three or four days old they should have their dew claws removed — a very simple operation if done by your vet when the puppies are very young. If this is forgotten, an adult dog can tear the leg during exercise. To remove them at a later stage takes longer and is more difficult, sometimes necessitating a general anaesthetic. So have the dew claws removed early and ask your veterinary surgeon to check the bitch over at the same time. She may also be given a calcium injection, which is beneficial to her and to the bone growth of the puppies.

Care of the puppies

If the bitch has a litter of five or more puppies it is as well to start them on solid food as early as three weeks old. This puts less strain on the mother. A teaspoonful of scrambled egg each is a good starter, as is Farex mixed with cow's milk and glucose or a tiny amount of minced meat given on the end of a finger. There are many brands of milk powder on the market and the puppies can be gradually taught to lap from this age onwards. By the time they are five weeks old they should be on five meals a day consisting of:

8 - 8.30am:	Farex with glucose and beaten egg yoke.
Midday:	Minced beef/chicken or fish with crumbled brown breadcrumbs or puppy meal covered with gravy.
3pm:	Scrambled egg. Mixed puppy milk.
6pm:	As for midday.
10pm:	Farex or Farley's Rusks dissolved in milk or porridge. A bowl of milk and another of water should be left with the puppies during the day and night.

By six weeks the puppies should be fully weaned and from five weeks the bitch will need to feed them only twice or three times a day, although — if she can be persuaded — she should stay with the litter at night. A separate basket of her own should be provided.

At four or five weeks the puppies should have their first worming dose, followed by a second after another two weeks. From eight weeks onwards they are old enough and strong enough to leave home. The buyer must be given a diet sheet, the puppy's Kennel Club registration certificate and a transfer of ownership form, as well as a pedigree. An application form to register a litter of puppies is obtainable from the Kennel Club who, on receipt of the completed form and registration fee, will return the certificates for the litter with the transfer forms. No puppy should be sold without these documents, and a pedigree, unless there is good reason for withholding them.

3

Coursing

Coursing is one of the most exciting of sports. As far back as Grecian times, the chronicler Flavius Arrianus (*AD* 150) devoted a whole book to the subject. There is enormous pleasure and pride in watching a dog using his brains, speed and turning powers in natural competition with his quarry. I think a good coursing dog gives one more satisfaction than a successful show or racing dog. The main pleasure stems from actually working one's dog, because coursing is the animal's instinctive exercise conducted in the natural environment of the countryside, as opposed to on an artificial track. To acquire an animal that excels at all three activities is the ultimate ambition of many Gazehound enthusiasts.

Most fair-minded people, having attended either Greyhound or Whippet coursing, will readily admit that the cruelty involved in any kill is reduced to the minimum. A hare that is quickly dispatched by a pair of hounds has a far better end than the one it would meet as a result of trapping or of a hare shoot. As has been repeatedly stressed to numerous investigators, the kill is not the ultimate aim or goal of a course. The purpose of a course is to test the relative merits of two Greyhounds in competitive rivalry for a hare. It is prowess not the killing itself that determines a coursing result.

In *Review of Coursing,* by Owen Stable *QC* and R. M. Stuttard, Section 165 on The Kill reads as follows:

In fact, a Kill is not the usual and typical end of a course. The statement by the British Field Sports Society, already referred to, says that the hare escapes in some 75% of cases. We think this is about right. In a record kept over two seasons covering 140 meetings of clubs in all parts of the country, it worked out that two in nine hares coursed were

31

killed, i.e. 22¾%, thus the chances in favour of the hare, taken over a season and allowing for all conditions, are between three and four to one. The rate will not be constant and will not necessarily hold for a particular area or meeting. Estimates made by clubs range from 5% to 30% killed and we ourselves have observed such a range. But we have also been present at a day's active and absorbing coursing when the hares were too much for every brace of dogs and not one was touched.

Mention is made in the same report of the type of death a hare might meet in other circumstances and an example is given of a farmer who found a hare with a broken jaw fourteen days after his hare shoot. The animal was dying a slow and unpleasant death from starvation.

It is not my intention to argue the rights and wrongs of the present anti-coursing campaign, but the subject must be mentioned because it could eventually alter the future of coursing. It is a sad, but undeniable, fact that originally most of the leaders of the campaign had never attended a coursing meeting. Despite this, they were hardly backward in voicing their loathing for what they termed a revolting and degenerate sport.

For those who don't know the rules of coursing and would like to read them, they are available from the National Coursing Club, which was formed in 1858. The rules run to more than fifty pages, so it would be wearisome to reprint them here. However, the original regulations drawn up at the time of Elizabeth I by the Duke of Norfolk are shorter and most interesting. They read as follows:

1. That he that is chosen Fewterer, or that lets loose the Greyhounds, shall receive the Greyhounds matched to run together, into his Leash, as soon as he comes into the field, and follow next to the hare-finder, or he who is to start the hare until he come unto the form; and no horseman of footman is to go before, or on any side, but directly behind, for the space of about forty yards.

2. You ought not to course a hare with more than a brace of Greyhounds.

3. The hare-finder ought to give the hare three so-ho's before he puts her from her form or seat, that the dogs may gaze about and attend her starting.

4. Twelve score yards law ought to be given before the dogs are loosed, unless there be danger of losing her.

5. The dog that gives the first turn, if after that there be neither cote, slip, nor wrench, wins the wager.

6. If the dog gives the first turn, and the other bears the hare, he that bears the hare shall win.

7. A go-by, or bearing the hare, is equivalent to two turns.

8. If neither dog turns the hare, he that leads last to the covert wins.

9. If one dog turns the hare, serve himself and turn her again, it is as much as a cote, and a cote is esteemed two turns.

10. If all the course be equal, he that bears the hare shall win, and if she be not borne, the course shall be adjudged dead.

11. If a dog takes a fall in a course, and yet performs his part, he may challenge the advantage of a turn more than he gave.

12. If a dog turns the hare, serve himself, and give divers cotes, and yet in the end stands still in the field, the other dog, if he turns home of the covert, although he gives no turn, shall be adjudged to win the wager.

13. If by misfortune a dog be ridden over in his course, the course is void, and to say the truth, he that did the mischief ought to make reparation for the damage.

14. If a dog gives the first and last turn and there be no other advantage between them, he that gives the odd turn shall win.

15. A cote is when a Greyhound goeth endways by his fellow and gives the hare a turn.

16. A cote serves for two turns, and two tripplings or jerkins for a cote; and if she turneth not right about she only wrencheth. The first version has it thus: A

cote shall be more than two turns, and a go-by, or
bearing the hare, equal to two turns.

17. If there be no cotes given between a brace of Greyhounds and that the one of them serves the other as
turning, then he that gives the hare most turns wins
the wager; and if one gives as many turns as the other,
he that beareth the hare wins the wager.

18. Sometimes the hare doth not turn but wrencheth, for
she is not properly said to turn, unless she turns, as it
were, round.

19. He that comes in first to the death of the hare, takes
her up and saves her from breaking, cherishes the dogs
and cleanses their mouths from the wool, is judged to
have the hare for his pains.

20. Those that are judges of the Leash must give their
judgement presently, before they depart the field.

These rules will, I hope, give some idea of the aim and
methods of conducting the sport. They applied naturally to
all Greyhound coursing, although there were various types of
Greyhounds at that time. It follows they were probably in use
for all Gazehound types.

Today, chasing Gazehounds all pursue the hare. Some
breeds imported to this country since Elizabethan times lack
their natural quarry so have had to become content with this
alternative. Salukis are the typical example, as they cannot
course the gazelle here. The Saluki Club has a coursing
section with rules based as nearly as possible on those of the
National Coursing Club, and about nine hare-coursing
meetings are held a year. Salukis do, of course, chase desert
hare in their natural habitat so the quarry is surely known to
them. Of the four coursing breeds used in this country,
Greyhounds are the fastest out of the slips, Salukis and
Deerhounds have the most stamina, and Whippets are more
agile on the turn.

For all breeds, the methods are the same and the meetings
are either walked up or driven. For the walked meeting the
owners and beaters advance in a straight line with the slipper
in a scarlet coat holding the two dogs in slips just ahead. The

judge is on a horse so that he can keep in touch with the dogs and assess their work. When the hare is put up by the line, the dogs are loosed.

For a driven event the slipper hides in front of a hedge or wall and the hares are driven from a field or wood behind him. When the hare emerges from the hedge and gets well ahead of the slipper (80 yards minimum start for Greyhound coursing) the dogs are released.

Each Hound wears a red or white collar, depending on how he is drawn. After the course the judge gives his decision, based on a points system for speed, turns, etc. He has a white and red flag which he waves to show which dog has won. The dogs are drawn in rounds or heats and there are upwards of three rounds per stake. Often the Hounds will overrun and disappear, particularly if a fresh hare is put up. They are allowed a thirty-minute breather before running again if they have won the previous round.

The intelligence and cunning of the hare should never be underestimated. In areas where they are coursed regularly (and this does happen in heavily poached parts of the country) they are tremendously fit and outpace the dogs with great ease. While Whippet coursing I have frequently noticed the hares change fields as the line of beaters approaches and, on some occasions on the Berkshire Downs, I have observed them watching the line below from a hill above and they have returned to the field once the beaters have moved.

The Waterloo Cup, the great event of the year for Greyhounds, was first run in 1836 as an eight-dog stake. A silver snuff-box was given to the winner, Lord Molyneux's Melanie. Molyneux was the son of Lord Sefton, whose family has been keenly interested in coursing ever since. Silver collars were also popular prizes at that time and an example can be seen in the early nineteenth-century painting by John Sherriff of Mountain Dew. It was on sale at the Tryon Gallery in about 1972. I have seen a rare collection of these collars in the possession of the family of the late Margaret Wigg. They are wide and extremely handsome and have the names of the winners engraved outside. Later, a cup was produced for the winner. Then in the 1930s £500 in prize money was added.

Today the winner receives £1,000.

The next year saw the start of the Altcar Plate (now the Waterloo Purse) and then finally the Waterloo Plate. The first coursing club, the Swaffham Coursing Club, was started in 1776 by the famous eccentric Lord Orford, who was also well known for the Greyhound/Bulldog cross he tried on his own stock. His intention was to increase the strength and determination of the Greyhound. Pictures of the crosses through the first, second and third generations are illustrated in most books on the breed, and the brindle colouring is said to derive from this experiment. During his long life, Lord Orford contributed much to the Greyhound and to coursing. Finally his mind failed, but just before his death he managed to escape the clutches of his family, who had him locked away, Brontë-fashion, and rode to see his Greyhound bitch, Czarina, run an important trial near Newmarket. As she won, he lifted his hat to her and fell off his pony, dead. A death many a sportsman would envy.

One of the most famous stories is told about a dog descended from Lord Orford's stock and belonging to Colonel Thornton from Yorkshire, who bought up most of the Orford Kennel. The dog was called Major and the story is told best by J. Wentworth Day in his book *The Dog in Sport:*

A Mr. Durand, who lived near Epsom, sent a challenge to Colonel Thornton for a thousand guineas, to match his Greyhound, Bellissima, against any of the Snowballs [a famous Greyhound family of which Major was one] 'Play or Pay'.

On the appointed day about five hundred people on horseback and as many again in carriages, whiskies, tax-carts, buggies, and other strange vehicles gathered on Sutton Heights to witness this momentous match.

The colonel, as usual, did things in terrific style. He was a great believer in pomp and majesty, and considered no-one more majestic than himself. Everything that could be done to impress was done on every possible occasion. So it was on this day.

First of all two of his retainers led out of the van two

brace of the Colonel's Greyhounds, sheeted in blue and buff. These were merely canine heralds for the dog Major, who then appeared in rich buff. On his right side was emblazoned the arms and crest of Colonel Thornton. On his left, in bold, gold lettering blazed the challenge, *'Major Aut Ne Plus Ultra'*, which, being modestly interpreted, means, 'There is nothing better than Major.'

Mr. Durand was overwhelmed. His heart, confidence, and his thousand guineas failed him on the spot. He announced that he was quite satisfied that no dog of his could possibly beat the magnificent Major. The match was off. The disappointment of the onlookers was prodigious. The Colonel scarcely concealed his disgust.

But Mr. Durand merely begged blandly that a box-hare should be liberated in order that the onlookers might see something of Major's powers. So the wretched box-hare was let loose. Major 'made a spring of many yards' and killed it. Whether this means that he took a standing leap immediately the hare dashed out of the box can best be left to the imagination.

A number of clubs were formed after the Swaffham Club, including the Malton and Ashdown Park clubs. By the middle of the nineteenth century there were 383 clubs but, as a result of a decrease in the number of hares on most estates after the Ground Game Act, there were only 137 clubs functioning by the end of the century. Today there are 25 Greyhound coursing clubs and 66 meetings are held during the year, making about 130 days coursing for Greyhounds alone. Whippets have about 36 days coursing per annum. Deerhounds about four and Salukis approximately nine. The season lasts from September to March.

The last three breeds win such trophies as cups and salvers for their achievements in the field, rather than prize money. The winning Whippets now have silver spoons — pure silver for the winner and silver plate for the runner-up. A trophy is also awarded in all three breeds to the dog who has won the most points during the season.

Despite the protests of the 'antis', there can be no substitute for hare coursing. It is a sport that it is impossible to simulate. There have been efforts to demonstrate the principal methods at country fairs where a drag has been used, but when testing a hound's ability to turn its quarry a drag cannot naturally respond. Similarly, an intelligent dog — Gazehounds *are* intelligent — is frequently uninterested in chasing a dummy animal. This has been proved on numbers of occasions in racing trials, particularly with dogs that have coursed live quarry at home. Numbers of really good coursing dogs simply will not chase an artificial lure.

A factor that can detract from the enjoyment of coursing is the risk of injury to one's dog from barbed wire, stubble and flints — to say nothing of the danger of traffic on busy side roads. Some coursing grounds have a road on at least one side of them and there must always be a risk that a hare will take the dogs across it. Every precaution is taken by the organisers to avoid these problems, but it is difficult to do so entirely. To counteract the risks, there is the thought that the hounds are doing what they most enjoy.

Finally, despite propaganda to the contrary, nothing gives the lover of sport greater satisfaction than to see the hare double back, redouble, then put on an extra burst of speed uphill to leave the dogs behind him.

4

Racing

GREYHOUNDS

Greyhound racing is a recent sport compared with the ancient coursing. The very first attempt to race took place in 1876, when a dummy hare was pulled by a sledge. America was the first country to see the tremendous potential in such a sport. It was introduced in Florida, where it immediately captured the imagination and interest of the public.

In 1926 Brigadier General Critchley, a Canadian, an American called Charlie Munn and Sir William Gentle persuaded friends to put up enough money to start a Greyhound track in this country. This was at Belle Vue Stadium, Manchester, and racing began in July 1926.

The first few meetings were not the immediate success that the promotors had hoped for, but by the fourth meeting attendance figures had risen to 15,000 — only 5,000 fewer than the 20,000 anticipated. Gradually the sport became economically viable. General Critchley and his American colleague then bought Harringay, which cost £150,000 to build. By that time there was no worry about whether or not racing would be a success. The White City opened in 1927.

The Greyhound Racing Association was formed before the first track was built. As racing became increasingly popular, more people bought dogs to take part in what had become the latest craze. The GRA opened training kennels where dogs were fed, trained and entered for races. They charged £1 per week.

Today, when one considers how much all prices have increased, the present charge must be considered very reasonable. Dogs are kept in stadium kennels now for about £5 a week, a fee which includes a free pass to all race meetings. The GRA now has its kennelling centre at Northaw in Hertfordshire, where close on 700 dogs are trained for the large London stadiums such as Harringay and Hackney. In future, Greyhound training will tend towards the American system: the trainer acquires his own kennels and staff and supplies dogs to race at the stadiums under contract.

In 1928 it was decided that the interests of the public must be protected, so the National Greyhound Racing Club was formed. The NGRC draws up all rules of racing and licenses all courses. It has often been described as the Jockey Club of Greyhound racing. Its original aims were to deal with the registration of all dogs on NGRC-approved courses and to have a method of identifying each one; to license all racecourses, all trainers and to produce a record of all dogs and officials registered with them. Before registering with the NGRC, a dog first has to be registered with the National Coursing Club. Each then receives a passport giving its markings, blemishes, weight, etc., and is checked against it at the traps and weigh-in before competing.

Entry to most of the big stadiums costs from about 25p to 70p, depending on where the spectator wants to be. There is betting on the totalisator and the bookmakers attend all meetings.

The usual distance for a Greyhound to run is 525 yards on an oval track. Over this they can average a speed of 36-37mph. The most important event of the Greyhound year is, of course, the Greyhound Derby, which attracts a crowd of around 40,000 despite the advent of television. The prize money for winning this race nowadays is around £12,000 and the lowest prize money for any win is £10. In addition, stud fees earned by a big winner are considerable. Patricia's Hope, the dog that won the Derby in 1972 and 1973, sired 400 puppies between the two races.

Buying a Greyhound is not as simple as it looks. A lot of prospective owners go to the Greyhound sales at Hackney or Aldridges and buy an adult that already has some form. Timed trials are run in the morning before the sale, so it is possible to look over the dog and also to see him run before making a bid. The dogs that do a slow or bad time can go for as little as £5 (but the novice who collects a good dog for that price is lucky indeed). To buy a tried dog of, say, two years old, direct from a trainer costs anything upwards from £150, probably much more. The prices at the sales can reach £2,000 and a really top-flight dog has been known to go for £8,000. But, on the other hand, one Derby winner cost only £60.

A greyhound starts its serious training at about fifteen months old, so it is possible to buy an untried dog of this age, but it would be wiser to purchase an animal that has done well in races at one of the smaller tracks and is capable of a time between 29.90 and 30sec. over the 525 yards. All stadium-trained dogs are graded by their trainer according to the times they achieve during their trials, so it is quite easy to find a good, average performer. Even if he won't win the Derby for his owner, he will provide sufficient entertainment.

It is possible to have a racer at a 'flapping track,' (one not recognised by the NGRC). However, if a Greyhound has been raced at one of these courses, he cannot compete on an NGRC-licensed track from then on. The standard at these tracks is not so high; some of the dogs are owner-trained and an animal suitable for this sort of competition is much less expensive. There are about eighty of these courses throughout the country.

Fans of the flapping tracks say that they would much rather train their own dogs, for they can then be sure that their dogs are never run unfit. They prefer to rear their own litters too, because they like the puppies to grow up in a family so that they show no nerves later on. Private trainers feel sure, when they give their dogs vitamins, wheat germ and other extras that they would not receive them at a stadium kennels.

Whatever an owner's beliefs, it is plainly more enjoyable for any dog to live in the family than to be kennelled with a number of others. There, are however, snags to the joys of the flapping track. One of these is that the NGRC tracks scrupulously take urine samples of the dogs before a big race to ensure that no dog competing has been doped. Although these tests are not conclusive, they are very nearly so, and the flapping tracks do not check the dogs in the same way. Greyhounds come from all parts of the country to race at flapping tracks and it would be comparatively simple to run a doped dog there, or even to switch dogs.

A moderate performer at a lesser track can help his owner financially. It can be bought for a reasonable sum, and, if it is home-trained, there will be no kennelling fees. The wins will, with luck, pay for keep and the owner can make extra with the bookies. Many owners are employed full-time doing everyday jobs, but the dogs are walked for an hour in the morning and then do about five miles in the evening. It must feel more than worthwhile to see a dog win that has been bred and trained at home.

In recent years attendance figures at all tracks have dropped. Televised football is probably the main counter-attraction. Even so, numbers still reach a total of 8 million a year. Some of the big stadiums have had to close down, others are fighting for survival. But it seems certain that the really well-run, large organisations will keep going.

WHIPPETS

This is an entirely different entertainment from Greyhound racing in that it is always strictly amateur. All dogs are owner-trained and most are house pets. The dogs that run with the only organisation for pure-bred dogs, the Whippet Club Racing Association, receive no cash prizes. It is very much a minority sport and practised by few, when compared with the enormous numbers of racing Greyhounds in training. Consequently there are no Whippet stadiums and no Whippet training kennels. The majority of clubs do their racing on what land is available. The equivalent of the size of a football pitch is all that is required. Meetings are held either on a straight course of 150 yards, or on an oval of 260 or 280 yards with two bends.

Undoubtedly the pioneer of Whippet racing in the South of

England was George McCourt of Totton in Hampshire. He was secretary of the New Forest Whippet Racing Club, which was the best-organised club south of Leicestershire and probably in the whole country. He was the first Racing Manager of the WCRA but unfortunately had to resign when he went to live in Germany. He introduced the present lure and track equipment used by the majority of southern Whippet racing clubs that copied his methods. The New Forest Club ran first at Stoney Cross near Cadnam, then at Totton football ground. Mr McCourt organised the major, South Coast Open Championship for several years running and this attracted competitors from all over the country. The New Forest was the first club to refuse dogs that were not Kennel Club registered. Until then, pure-bred Whippet racing was invaded by Lurchers, in the shape of Greyhound and Terrier crosses, which built up considerable resentment among the owners of pedigree dogs. These non-pedigree animals continue to race, but under the auspices of a separate organisation, so the racing scene has improved considerably as a result. The WCRA is opposed to cash prizes as it feels that they open the sport to dishonesty in the shape of ringing and interference with the lure — among other practices.

The Whippet Club Racing Association was formed by a sub-committee of the senior breed club, the Whippet Club. Like the NGRC it has drawn up rules of racing enforced at all championship meetings held by the association. Only dogs that have obtained Class 1 Kennel Club registration are eligible to apply to be registered with the WCRA, but, even then, not all are necessarily accepted. The final decision on whether a dog may race with the association or not rests with the registrar, who issues passports almost identical to those used by the NGRC. Each book gives the Kennel Club number and details of breeding, colour, weight etc. The markings of the dog are filled in, in exactly the same way as in the Greyhound books and the dogs are checked at the weigh-in before running at a WCRA meeting.

The association runs four championship meetings a year. Some are held at a central track, others are organised by the

clubs affiliated to the WCRA on their home tracks. Conditions must meet the association's requirements, which are
modelled as nearly as possible on the rules of the European
organisation, the Union Internationale des Clubs de Lévriers.
For the meetings that are held on an oval track, a Continental
plan adapting the layout of the European track to the size of
a football ground is used. The lure is worked by a battery-
powered motor; the traps are modelled on Greyhound ones
and must work from a central point so that the front opens in
one piece. The dogs run in the same colours as Greyhounds
and wear muzzles to prevent fighting over the lure at the end
of the race.

Whippets run in weight classes and must be entered
correctly before a championship meeting. They are weighed
before racing. There are eight weight classes ranging from 16
to 30lb. No dog weighing over 30lb may race, nor may any
animal over 21 in. in height. Races are run on a time- or
weight-handicap system by many racing clubs, in order to
vary the results a little and give some encouragement to the
owners of mediocre dogs. Obviously a championship meeting
could not be run this way, because the best dogs are
frequently handicapped out of the race, but it is much more
interesting at club meetings if every dog is given a chance of
winning.

The WCRA gives the title of Whippet Club Racing
Champion to any dog that has won two championship finals.
To date, there are nearly 700 dogs registered with the
association and thirty racing champions. To win a championship final is difficult, as a dog has first to win a heat, then the
semi-final, before it competes in the final. Each champion
receives a certificate and each finals winner an embroidered
coat and a plaque or shield.

When the Association started, it was supported by southern
clubs only. This was because the majority of pure-bred
Whippet enthusiasts came from the South, and the North
continued to run their cross-breeds. Strangely enough, it is
comparatively recently that serious Northern and Midlands
breeders have started to take interest in Whippet racing. The
Tamworth Club in Staffordshire has now joined, to represent

the Midlands, and there are signs that certain clubs in the North will follow.

Only clubs are allowed to join the WCRA — owners and dogs are not members. Each dog is registered through the club his owner joins. Thus an owner who is not a member of a club affiliated to the association cannot apply to register his dog.

Puppies may not race at a WCRA championship meeting until twelve months old. Previously, puppies had been competing in races against adults at the age of five months, a practice deplored by the WCRA since no hound finishes its growing until it is at least fifteen months old. Unfortunately, this malpractice is still allowed in some racing clubs, particularly if the owners have not had sufficient experience to see the results of their actions.

Each year racing registrations increase, so Whippet racing, which started originally at the end of the last century and revived dramatically ten years ago, appears to be here to stay. Improvement of racing ruling, track conditions and equipment are all very much in the minds of the enthusiasts. When funds reach the necessary figure the association intends to build a track exclusively for its championship meetings, with permanent equipment installed so that the sport is run at the highest possible amateur level, as on the Continent. The present secretary of the WCRA is: Mrs Peter Spokes, 3 Stockwell Furlong, Haddenham, Aylesbury, Bucks., and the registrar is: Mrs Ian Lowe, Far End, Kingham, Oxon.

AFGHANS

This is an innovation and again is run in conjunction with a breed club — the Afghan Hound Association. The dogs run over varying distances at Blindley Heath in Surrey and Hinckley in the Midlands. Further details are given in the chapter on this breed. The Afghan Hound Association has a list of rules which, unlike the Greyhound and Whippet rulings, is not too long to print and will be of interest to followers of the Afghan. The list reads as follows:

Afghan Hound Association Racing Rules

1. Only pure-bred, Kennel Club-registered Afghan hounds are eligible to race at AHA race meetings. If there should be some reason for doubt, a complaint should be lodged with the Racing committee, after which the dog in question may not be raced at any subsequent meeting until its Kennel Club registration certificate has been seen by the racing committee.

2. All dogs and bitches to be raced must be over twelve months of age and not exceeding 7 years of age (without permission of the racing committee) and should, of course, be fit.

3. All bitches in season or whelp are excluded from racing.

4. Any owner or handler may enter his/her Afghan in a novice (Green) race, but only A.H.A. members may race their dogs for the further awards of merit. Membership cards to be shown at race meetings.

5. Muzzles must be worn by dogs and bitches at all times when racing.

6. Not more than 4 dogs to be run in each race.

7. Any dog causing interference to other entrants is automatically disqualified, except in Green and Yellow star races. Dogs previously disqualified for interference shall be barred from further racing, except solo, at the discretion of the Racing Committee and by their permission only. Persistent interference barred absolutely.

8. Any one dog past the start marker constitutes a race. In this case no re-run will be allowed.

9. In all trapped races the dogs must be completely trapped, with the doors closed and the handlers away from the traps.

10. The time of all trapped races will be taken from the time the traps open until the dogs pass the finishing line.

11. It is the responsibility of the individual to have his or her dog in the marshalling ring whilst the preceeding race is in progress.

12. The appropriate qualification certificate must be produced at the time of booking the race.

13. Owners and handlers must collect their dogs immediately the race is finished.

14. No dog or bitch shall compete in races totalling more than 1,500 yards at any one meeting without special permission of the Racing Committee.

15. It is the responsibility of owners or handlers to have their dogs under control at all times.

16. It is suggested that owners do not let their dogs eat or drink prior to racing.

17. The Racing Committee reserve the right to refuse permission to race.

18. Any objection, as a result of a race, must be lodged with a member of the Racing Committee within 15 minutes of the incident. The decision of the Racing Committee is final.

5

Showing

For those readers who neither show nor understand the show system this chapter outlines the basic principles.

All dog shows — with the exception of a few of the exemption variety — are held under the rules of the governing body, the Kennel Club. Exemption Shows normally hold some classes for pedigree dogs and others for pet owners and child handlers. They are usually organised for a charity, or in conjunction with a village fête or agricultural show. There are various types of shows for pure-bred dogs, starting with a match in which various breeds of dogs are drawn in pairs to compete against each other. As one is knocked out from each pair, the remaining dog goes on to the next round until the eventual winner emerges from the last two animals.

A sanction show is open to dogs from puppy, maiden, novice, junior, tyro, graduate and post-graduate classes. Maiden classes are for dogs which have not won a first prize, novice for dogs that have not won more than three first prizes, and so on up the scale. So no dog may compete at a sanction show if it has won five or more first prizes of £1 or more in post-graduate or any higher class, such as limit or open. All exhibitors at a show must be a member of the society organising it.

Limited shows are again open only to members of the club or society concerned, but dogs may compete that have won prizes from puppy up to open class, although no animal is eligible for a limited show if it has won a challenge certificate or any award towards a championship title.

Open shows are open to all people and all dogs, regardless of their previous wins or whether or not they are members of a canine society.

Championship Shows are the most important type from the

Above, Miss Niblock's Afghan Hound, Champion Khanabad White Warrior, winner of a hound group and five challenge certificates; *below*, Afghans in action on the race track

Above, a group of Miss Marilyn Willis' Springett Borzois; *below* a successful Borzoi waits to receive his racing trophy

Above, Miss Anastasia Noble's Deerhound, Champion Aurora of Ardkinglas, a show champion and coursing stake winner; *below*, Champion Fitzroy of Ardkinglas, owned by Miss Noble and the son of Champion Aurora, pictured above

Above, Mrs. Wilton-Clark's Champion Shalfleet Sir Lancelot, who holds the breed record by winning eighteen challenge certificates and won the hound group at Cruft's in 1973; *below,* a Greyhound at full stretch.

point of view of the really serious exhibitor, because a
challenge certificate for dogs and bitches is generally on offer
for most breeds. Furthermore, the classification at these
shows is more generous. Only the poorly supported breeds
(those that have very few registrations recorded at the Kennel
Club) do not have challenge certificates offered at the
majority of such shows.

To become a champion, a dog has to win three challenge
certificates (referred to hereafter as CCs or tickets) under
three different judges. This is not as easy as it might seem.
Firstly, the dog must win his class, and in the open class he
will often be competing against a number of champions.
Having achieved this, he then has to go back into the ring
and compete against all other unbeaten dogs. If the judge
decides he is the best specimen of all the class winners the CC
is awarded to him — provided it is decided that he is worthy
of it. CCs are not often withheld, but it has been known to
happen. The reserve best dog is awarded the reserve CC. In
big breeds this is no mean achievement as it indicates that the
dog is reserve best out of perhaps 200 entries.

Another Kennel Club award is the junior warrant which
can be won by a young dog or bitch between the ages of six
and eighteen months. No dog can be exhibited before the age
of six months. To win this award, 25 points must be gained
and only first prizes count towards it. Three points are given
for every first won at a championship show and one for a win
at an open show.

At championship shows all breeds are classified in groups,
such as the Gundog group, the Terrier group, the Toy group,
the Working group, the Utility group and the Hound group.
The latter comprises the Gazehounds and other hounds, such
as Beagles, Bassets, Dachshunds, etc. When the challenge
certificates have been awarded, the judge decides between the
dog and bitch winners for his best-of-breed award. The
winner of this then goes forward to compete against the other
hounds in the Hound group, and this winner then competes
against the last five dogs for the best-in-show trophy.

There are twenty-eight championship shows a year — not
including breed-club shows. In a well-supported breed —

such as Afghans and Whippets — with three or more major breed clubs, there would be a chance of approximately thirty CCs to be won a year. The less-popular breeds, however, such as Greyhounds, have a much less generous classification and only some twelve CCs on offer each year.

Notices of future shows are published in the canine press, namely the magazines *Dog World, Our Dogs* and *The Kennel Gazette,* printed by the Kennel Club. Further help for novices is available from breed-club secretaries, whose names and addresses can be supplied by the Kennel Club.

The most important show of the year is undoubtedly Cruft's, although now, because of the qualification ruling, it is not necessarily the biggest. Even before exhibits at Cruft's had to qualify to go to the show, the Ladies Kennel Association and Richmond Championship Show packed more dogs into Olympia in a single day than Cruft's ever did. Nevertheless, it still draws the biggest crowd of all, partly because of its early history and foundation by the late Charles Cruft at the end of the last century, and partly because of all shows, it is the only one which really attracts the foreign buyers.

Over the last seven years it has been promoted to an all-quality show in that all dogs entered have to have won major prizes at a championship show during the previous year. In 1973 the results of a revised qualifier, which brought the numbers down to the ideal figure sought after by the Cruft's show committee, became apparent. In 1972 there had been far too drastic a decrease as first-prize winners only were allowed to compete. In 1973 the classification and qualification rules were changed so that only first-prize winners from the medium-grade classes — such as novice and postgraduate — could compete, but first and second placings were allowed from puppy, junior and limit classes, and first, second and third prize winners from the open classes because the latter usually contain the cream of all exhibits. Each year there is usually some further change to the qualification system.

All breeds suffer to a certain degree from this ruling. In the popular breeds, the classes are enormous and can consist of anything up to forty competitors. The chances of being placed in the first two in classes of this size are not remote, but, in puppy classes particularly, the first two places are frequently taken by the same two exhibits at each show. At the other end of the scale, Greyhounds, for example, do not even have classes at every championship show. They have to compete in variety classes, although the exhibits entered will be considerably fewer when they do have a classification.

However, the Cruft's committee undoubtedly had to reduce numbers at the show, or extend it to three days, which is difficult to organise. The problems of hygiene alone in running an indoor dog show over three days would daunt the bravest of committees.

One of the best run and most enjoyable championship shows is the large West of England Ladies Kennel Society Show. This has been held for many years in the grounds of Boddington Manor near Cheltenham, but in 1975 the venue was changed to Circencester Park. Attractive surroundings, coupled with the fact that it is the first of the open-air shows, are added attractions. It must rate high on the list of most exhibitors.

The Three Counties Show, held in the Vale of the Malvern Hills, is another extremely popular show. It is run in conjunction with one of the largest agricultural shows, and this provides added interest and entertainment. Nevertheless, the open shows and the breed-club shows are the most relaxed and pleasurable. The pressure is not on to the same degree, the standard is frequently very high, and the atmosphere more relaxed.

Today, showing is expensive and consequently its popularity never ceases to be surprising, for the prize money is small. Cruft's pay £4 for a first prize, £2 for second prize and £1 for third prize. The usual championship-show prize money is £2 for a first, £1 for a second and 50p for a third. In view of the fact that many canine societies have increased their entry fee to £2 per dog per class, there isn't a hope of showgoers even covering expenses. Even if they win a first prize their petrol, car park and catalogue charges remain as unpaid overheads. Unless they win a major award — such as a puppy stakes (usually promoted by sponsors) which is worth about £5 to the winner — they will finish considerably out of pocket at the end of the day. In view of increased running costs, Richmond Championship Show Committee decided to give prize cards only, and no prize money, for their 1975 show and there is a strong possibility that other canine societies will follow their example. If this happens the exhibitors will have no hope at all of recovering expenses.

Undoubtedly showing promotes sales of both puppies and adult dogs. A regular and successful exhibitor has much more chance of selling the progeny of show-winning parents than has the breeder of a litter bred from dogs that are kept simply as pets. A successful show dog or champion can be sold for four-figure sums if the owner is prepared to part with him.

Most exhibitors show because they enjoy it and find it fascinating to continue trying to breed a dog to beat all other contestants. It is also of great interest to see what type of stock is produced by combining certain bloodlines. One of the most frequent criticisms levelled at the Cruft's committee was that, because of the qualifier, new puppies from six to nine months would not have a chance to qualify. Consequently, puppy classes, so interesting to regular exhibitors and foreign buyers, would have very few entries.

As to showing methods, Gazehounds are usually easy subjects because they don't need the same amount of preparation as other breeds. Only the Afghan has a really long coat to groom. Borzois need similar treatment but to a lesser extent. The remaining six breeds are not too difficult to keep in glowing show condition.

Furthermore, Gazehounds have suffered much less from the quirks of show fashion than other groups — Gundogs, for instance. This is paradoxical because there is an abundance of work for a good Retriever. Yet the natural quarry of so many Gazehounds is not available to him, either for legal or for environmental reasons. Nevertheless, many hound owners are great sporting enthusiasts, so as a group these dogs are worked consistently and hereditary defects are few, even to the point of being almost nonexistent.

To show any breed of hound before a judge it is necessary to stand it naturally, with the front feet straight but slightly apart and level. The hindquarters must be at a natural angle without being bunched up or stretched out too far behind. If this is practised from the time it is a small puppy of five or six weeks, the dog will never forget his training. With the smaller hounds, it is frequently necessary to stand them on a table so that the judge can go over them more easily. In these cases the training can be started when the dogs are being groomed on a table.

All exhibits are expected to walk up and down at a fairly smart pace on a lead, so that the judge can assess movement. It is necessary to run the larger hounds, otherwise they cannot be expected to stride out as they should. Judges sometimes prefer the dog to be moved in a triangle, but the exhibitor must watch and see what is asked of other exhibitors before his or her turn comes. Before being moved away, every dog is examined and when each has been thoroughly assessed all exhibits are expected to line up together so that the judge can make his placings.

Although the immediate preparation of most hounds is simple, for as working dogs they must be in hard, physical condition which takes considerable effect over the long term, it is still always an arguable point as to how much muscle should be allowed on a shoulder. A good judge should be able to distinguish between a shoulder that is a little too heavy from exercise and the congenitally coarse shoulder, often with a short blade, that worsens after coursing or racing.

To show a Gazehound in peak condition, you must have him fit and with coat gleaming. Whippets, Greyhounds and Pharaoh Hounds just need brushing and a final rub with a silk scarf. The feathering on the quarters and tail sometimes needs a little trimming with nail or hairdresser's scissors, but on no account should the whiskers be trimmed on any dog: they act as antennae and allow animals to gauge the width of a gap or opening in a wall or hedge. Deerhounds, Wolfhounds and Borzois need regular brushing, preferably with a rubber or bristle brush, and combing, so that the curlier coat round the legs, tail and quarters is kept free of knots and tangles. Afghans are the only difficult members of the Gazehound group, because their coats are so profuse, but as long as they are groomed thoroughly and regularly, a metal comb and bristle brush before they go into the ring should do the trick. It should not be necessary to use scissors, except when the hair is very matted. A little water on the coat often helps to remove tangles and, of course, any dog must be cleaned after a muddy walk.

Teeth must be kept clean and it is a very simple matter to chip the tartar from the eye and other teeth by using a sterilised blunt instrument and scraping downwards away from the gums. If the dog shows any sign of having an infected or painful tooth this work should not be done at home and veterinary advice must be sought. Old dogs should be taken regularly to have their teeth scraped professionally, as bad teeth can cause both infections and kidney problems.

For many breeds it is fashionable to cut the nails down almost to the quick. This is quite incorrect for a running hound, which must have enough on the end of the nail to grip the ground when running.

Bathing is another essential if a dog is to be kept in good coat, but too many baths can dry the coat. A good canine shampoo should always be used.

Showing can become very dispiriting to the novice exhibitor, as it takes time and experience to learn how to handle an exhibit to its best advantage, but perseverance is the sensible course of action. Only by looking at dogs, does one learn to pick out good and bad points of conformation and the art of handling.

There are other points too about show-ring behaviour which it is as well to know. It is not done to speak to the judge unless he asks a question about the exhibit. Bitches in season should not be shown, as they unsettle the dogs on the benches and in the ring. There is no rule against it, but it is very unpopular with other exhibitors. Even when dogs and bitches are shown separately, a bitch in this condition could well be benched next to a dog that may damage himself in trying to scale the partition next to her. Another unpopular habit is to show a dog bred by the judge.

None of the hound breeds is measured or weighed, as happens with such breeds as Dachshunds and Poodles. Most of the hound-breed clubs feel that a dog's height can be measured differently by several judges, and there is also the fact that the hound's height varies when he is either tense or relaxed. An excited or nervous animal will stand right up on his toes and increase his height by up to half an inch. Another factor is that, at outside shows, one can rarely depend on the ground being level. Many dogs react adversely to measuring on a table, so on the ground is the only answer. Occasionally a special prize is offered at breed-club shows for the best dog or bitch less than a certain height and in this case a dog must obviously be measured. Most judges should be able to assess a dog's height without a measure anyway. All the breed standards give a recommended height and the final decision on this very controversial question must rest with the judge.

It is difficult for even the most experienced of exhibitors to know if his dog is up to show standard until he is standing in the ring with other exhibits. Only by comparison can one tell whether or not one's animal has potential. Obviously it's a waste of time to show a dog with a bad mouth — either undershot or overshot — as this is a really major fault. There are few judges who do not check the dog's mouth before going over him. Occasionally, an inexperienced judge may omit to inspect the animal's teeth, but this is very unusual. A dog with an incorrect bite could never have a successful show career. It is also unwise to show a dog that is not entire. Entire means that he has both testicles fully descended. A dog that has either one or no testicles is called either a monorchid or a crytorchid. Although there is no longer a Kennel Club rule to say that one may not exhibit a dog that is not entire, few judges would place one.

Finally, all exhibitors should go to a show equipped with, as well as the brush and comb previously mentioned, a well-fitting collar, a strong lead to tether the dog to the bench and a pin for the exhibit's number card.

Showing can be interesting and it must give breeders immense satisfaction to take a home-bred dog to the very top. One should, however always keep a sense of proportion on the subject, as it is, after all, secondary to real sport.

6

The Afghan

Alphabetically the Afghan rightly heads the Gazehound group, but the breed has other claims to precedence. The Afghan is numerically the most popular sighthound in the English show world if the Kennel Club registration figures and show entries are taken as a guide.

As is the case with so many animals, the historian has to rely on art sources, albeit primitive ones, to identify the Afghan's progenitors. But, in common with the Irish Wolfhound, there is little or no proof of his existence until the beginning of the last century. Unlike the Wolfhound, the Afghan is not a made breed (by this one means a breed that is a product of environment and natural genetics and not one brought about by the contrivance of man). So it is particularly surprising that, apart from a single manuscript in the Bodleian Library in Oxford, which depicts hounds resembling Afghans, there are no paintings or drawings of these dogs until the famous drawing, executed in 1813, of the Meenah of Jaijurh with his Afghan.

Obviously these hounds are closely related to the Saluki. It is supposed that the heavy coat developed to suit the extremes of climate in the mountains of Afghanistan, thereby particularly distinguishing it from the Saluki. Nevertheless, if the Jaijurh drawing is correct, either the Meenah is exceptionally tall or his Afghan is far smaller than the average Saluki. However, Oriental tradition makes the principal character in a picture physically larger than his associates or other subjects. In this case, the man might well be interpreted as superior in rank to the dog. Furthermore, one of the earliest imports to this country a century later, Sirdar of Ghazni, was reputed to be only 24in. high, so the scale of the picture might be correct.

There is a celebrated and romantic theory that there was an Afghan among the animals in Noah's Ark. This has been suitably exploded by Hope and David Waters in their book *The Saluki in History, Art and Sport*. They say that the Saluki is the oldest of the Greyhound family. It is sometimes claimed that the Afghan hound has this distinction and that it entered the Ark with Noah. But it is in Babylonian and Assyrian literature that a long account of the Great Deluge has been found, the best known being Tablet II of the *Epic of Gilgamesh*. But this discovery is geographically outside Afghanistan and linguistically associated with a different culture. Also the latest archeological opinion interprets this written evidence as pointing to the flood stories having originated with the melting of the ice fields at the end of the last glacial period. In the Near East this occurred about 10,000*BC*. As radio-carbon dating of archeological material from the Fertile Crescent puts the beginning of civilization at about 9,000*BC*, the memory of the floods would have been comparatively recent in this region. The fact that no tradition of a great flood is found in Egypt, which, because of its geographical position would have escaped the worst, lends support to this interpretation. Afghanistan is a land in which no ancient civilisation flourished. No indigenous archaeological remains of great antiquity have yet been discovered. Geographically it is not favourably sited for the early development of civilisation.

After giving further historical and geographical evidence to support the premise, the Waters go on to say:

Until the last quarter of the nineteenth century the Afghan hound was unknown in Europe, was rarely found far from the frontiers of its native habitat, and has not been found represented in painting, fresco or relic. There are thus sound reasons for continuing to believe with the archaeologists that the Saluki is the progenitor of coursing hounds and is thousands of years older than the Afghan hound. It is most probable that the latter derives from the Saluki, having been brought into Afghanistan (where the Saluki, is still found) with caravans plying between the ancient civilizations of the Fertile Crescent and the Indus Valley, or in search of gold, copper or lapis lazuli from Afghanistan itself, and there developed by selective breeding into a hound well suited to the mountainous terrain and prey pursued in Afghanistan.

This latter point is of interest because, although all the experts agree that there is a direct relationship between the two breeds, it is nevertheless remarkable that Saluki characteristics could be altered and developed so readily to suit exactly the opposite type of terrain from which it had hitherto been used. One associates the Afghan with the steep, rocky surface of the mountains and hills of Afghanistan. To negotiate these successfully, he requires tremendously powerful quarters, well-rounded feet with large, strong pads and less length of loin than the Saluki. Mrs Amps, one of the first people to bring an Afghan to Britain, wrote in the magazine *Our Dogs* that Afghans near the Indian frontier were occasionally crossed with Salukis in order to reduce the coat. She goes on to claim that the best strains (i.e. those from the Afghanistan hills) had a really exceptionally heavy coat to withstand the harsh climate there. The fact that the occasional Afghan litter is born short-coated indicates that a close-coated dog, such as the Saluki, must have been a predecessor.

The story of the Afghan's introduction to Britain has been dealt with extensively in several books. As already mentioned, two distinct types were imported just after the First World War. It is from these that the modern dog, as recognised in the West, has emerged. Colonel and Mrs Bell-Murray brought a dozen Afghans here from the plains of Afghanistan. These were light in coat and racey in outline, with particularly attractive heads. A few years later, Colonel and Mrs Amps brought their 'of Ghazni' dogs into the country and among these was Sirdar of Ghazni, later an English champion, who was bred in the king's kennels in Afghanistan. He and the other hounds from this kennel were smaller and stockier than the Bell-Murray dogs, with much heavier coats.

The first Afghan champions, Buckmal and Ranee, both gained their titles in 1927 and came from the Bell-Murray breeding, despite Mrs Amps's articles and verbal statements at that time that they were not of a truly correct type. However, Colonel Amps was commissioned to buy all the Maharajah of Patiala's Afghan hounds and was probably the most knowledgeable man on the subject in the Far East.

In August 1971, Mr Alan Mytton went on a tour of Afghanistan and was asked by Afghan-hound enthusiasts to photograph Afghans in their native surroundings. The result was a picture reproduced in the Afghan Hound Association's magazine *Think Afghan*. It shows a hound remarkably like those imported by Colonel Bell-Murray with a long — though not exaggerated — coat, a ringed tail, low-set ears and well-developed deep brisket. However, this does not imply that the Amps's type is not competitive with the Bell-Murray type. Sirdar of Ghazni, as stated, had a remarkable and desirable effect on the breed. Yet the trade-press polemics delivered by Mrs Amps to support her breeding does not do justice to the contribution of the Bell-Murrays.

The original purpose for which these dogs were used was coursing the snow leopard, the jackal and the hare in the Afghanistan mountains and for guarding the nomadic native tribes and their sheep and goats. To this day, there are annual events at which dogs and goats are brought down from the mountains for local fêtes. For the duration of the festival, the hounds are garlanded with bright-blue necklaces of the national stone and necklets of flowers.

One of Mrs Amps's imports was said to have killed a leopard that was carrying off one of her puppies. Sir Evelyn Cobb, who helped Mrs Amps with her first imports, said in correspondence on the subject in *The Field* magazine (19 October 1967) that the dogs he saw in Afghanistan were used primarily for coursing the Asiatic hare or Persian gazelle. He went on to say that British show specimens are bigger and heavier than their progenitors, as a result of selective breeding for show rather than for coursing.

Since the days of the first imports, the Afghan's popularity has increased to a fantastic extent. At most championship shows he tops the hound entries. At the Hound Association shows, for hound breeds only, Afghans usually head the entry by a hundred or more and the Kennel Club registration figures for the breed have been increasing at the rate of nearly a thousand a year. The senior breed club, the Afghan Hound Association has about a thousand members under its secretary, Mrs Ann Adams of the Badakshan prefix.

Undoubtedly Afghans are beautiful, striking animals, but they take up a large amount of space, their coats need ceaseless grooming and the average owner does not buy an Afghan with a view to using it for sporting purposes. Their popularity, therefore is difficult to understand, although I suspect that their spectacular appearance has contributed very largely to the number of show kennels that have turned to the Afghan rather than to any other breed.

Regrettably they are to be seen all too often in the company of models or starlets with whom they are presumably leading a cramped life in a London flat. The breed clubs are extremely worried about the breed's popularity and Mr David Paton, until 1973 the very able secretary of the AHA, had this to say on the breed in the club magazine:

Everyone must face the fact that the breed has reached saturation point. There were never enough homes of the right kind and now there are too many puppies on the market unable to get homes of any kind. And some people's animals are having several litters at a time and getting stuck with them. There are so many misconceptions. People who use a champion dog so often think that all the pups will turn out perfect show dogs, which is usually completely wrong. The whole situation is a sad one and there seem to be all too many Afghan owners who are wilfully careless of the ultimate fate of the puppies they breed. Of course many breeders are truly concerned, as your Committee is, and try to spread sensible counsel. The Code of Ethics which has so far been signed by 117 people, is a good guideline to the sort of conduct the AHA would like to see become general. I hope more people will come both to read and abide by it.

The 'code of ethics' mentioned by Mr Paton sets out fifteen

recommendations on the breeding, rearing and selling of Afghans. Other breed clubs would do well to follow the Association's example.

The breed clubs are well aware that, with any popular breed, faults of conformation are bound to occur. Recently, shoulders have been sharply criticised, the main complaint being that shoulder blades are either too straight or too short so that the Afghan's front, and front action, are affected. A short blade can unbalance the whole outline of an animal and restrict stride so that it lacks the length and freedom it should have. Breed experts feel that there is not enough angulation of the blade, which should lie at an angle of 45°. Heads are another arguing point: if they are too wide at the top this can coarsen the head and expression, but if they get too much the other way a narrow head and muzzle can produce weak jaws. Either fault can alter the set of the eyes, which can change the animal's whole appearance. Coats must not become so excessively long that they mask the general outline. One of the characteristics of the Afghan is a saddle of shorter hair and when the coat becomes too profuse this feature disappears entirely. Probably in no other breed is there such owner awareness of the danger in numbers: every effort is made to guide the inexperienced during teach-ins; detailed discussions on the breed standard are given both in breed magazines and the dog press.

The first race meetings for Afghans were organised in 1968 by the Afghan Hound Association at Blindley Heath in Surrey, where the dogs race on sand. Now they also race at Hinckley in the Midlands on a turf surface. The present racing is conducted over 300 yards, 500 yards and 710 yards at Hinckley; and 400 yards, 760 yards and 1,120 yards at Blindley Heath. Coloured certificates are awarded to the dogs at Hinckley and these are given on timing. Green certificates are presented to those that cover the 300 yards in 25 sec., yellow for 24.5sec., blue for 24sec. and red for 23.5sec. A silver star of merit is given to the dog that covers 500 yards in 39.50sec. or less and 710 yards in 55.50sec. Racing is held on the third Sunday of every month throughout the summer at Hinckley and every second Sunday at Blindley

Heath. Competitors come to race from as far away as Scotland and the popularity of the sport has doubled in the last five years. All racing dogs must be Kennel Club registered.

As a result of the large number of Afghans in this country and the fact that there are nine breed clubs, it is very difficult to single out one kennel for mention before another. The Afghan has had a fair share of show triumphs. At Cruft's in 1953, for example, Mrs Morton's Champion Netheroyd Alibaba, was reserve best in show all breeds. Mrs Jo Holden's Ch. Ranjitsinhji of Jagai was best in show all breeds at Richmond Show in 1968 and Mrs Dods's Champion Horningsea Tiger's Eye, one of the breed's greatest sires, was best in show at the Hound Association show in 1969. The same owner's Champion Horningsea Khanabad Suvaraj, bred by Miss Niblock, was Dog of the Year in 1962, with numerous group wins, and was the sire of the late Mrs Race's litter brother and sister, Ch. Rifka's Tabac d'Rar and Ch. Musquat d'Rar (this holds the breed record of twenty challenge certificates). In 1973, the top winning dog, the Rev. Ford and Miss Helen Barnes's Afghan dog the late Ch. Hajubah of Davlen was best in show all breeds at Cardiff championship show. In both 1974 and 1975 Mrs Anna Paton's bitch Ch. Amudarya Khala achieved group and best-in-show wins.

I have deliberately mentioned only the winners of this type of top award, but credit should go to Miss Jennifer Dove, who at only sixteen years old, bred her first litter and produced Ch. Saringa's Abracadabra. She claims to be the youngest owner/breeder of a champion Afghan.

The breed clubs not only work extremely hard to resolve the problem of the numbers of Afghans, but they also try to ensure that only the best judges should appear on their lists. For example, the Afghan Hound Association, in common with most breed clubs, has an A, B and C judging list. The A list is for junior judges only. Before adding his or her name to the list, the association gives the prospective judge a practical test, in which he or she handles and places three or four Afghans provided by the AHA committee. While handling them, the judge must give an opinion about each point of conformation and give his or her reasons for the order in which they are placed. Subsequently the judge is questioned by the board, which consists of the Afghan Hound Association chairman, a championship show judge from the committee and three other championship show judges who are members of the club. After this, the judge is deemed suitable to judge five classes at limit or open shows. When he has two years of sufficient experience behind him, he may then qualify for the B list which allows him to judge up to ten classes at open or limit shows. The C list is for those able to award challenge certificates.

The Southern Afghan Club has devised a similar scheme and a programme to help all breed judges. This consists of a series of lectures by breed specialists on conformation and bone construction, among other subjects. After each lecture, those candidates wishing to be awarded a judging diploma undergo a written and practical examination.

The Afghan standard was adopted by the Kennel Club in 1950, but was based on the Afghan standard drawn up in 1925, which used the famous dog, Zardin, as a model. Zardin was brought to Britain in 1907 by Captain John Barff and was shown at a championship show at Crystal Palace, where he won the class for foreign exhibits. Queen Alexandra invited him to Buckingham Palace and he made a tremendous impression on the British show scene. Unfortunately he was later sold to a dealer and faded into obscurity, leaving no progeny to perpetuate his name. But his photograph and a detailed description remained and, when a standard was first discussed in 1912, he was the best example of the breed available. He was a pale colour with a very heavy coat and a beautiful head. It was a tragedy that he had no descendants.

The standard states under characteristics: 'The Afghan Hound should be dignified and aloof, with a certain keen fierceness. The Eastern or Oriental expression is typical of the breed. The Afghan looks at and through one.' It is this last sentence which typifies everything we know of the Afghan and, as long as his dignity and beauty are preserved, he must continue to flourish.

The names and addresses of the breed clubs and their secretaries are as follows:

Afghan Hound Association
Mrs Ann Adams, Cockle Point, Marine Walk, Hayling Island, Hants, PO11 9PQ.

Southern Afghan Club
Mrs D. M. Gie, West Down, Hastingleigh, Nr Ashford, Kent.

Nothern Afghan Hound Society
Mrs J. van Schaick, Alicia Cottage Kennels, Rochdale, Lancashire.

Midland Afghan Hound Club
Mrs N. Thorpe, Midway House, Baidegate Lane, Hickling Pastures, Melton Mowbray, Leicestershire.

Western Afghan Hound Club
Mrs C. A. Hill, 3 The Nydon, Catcott, Nr Bridgewater, Somerset.

Afghan Hound Club of Wales
Mrs F. Whiteley, The Rock, St Mary Hill, Bridgend, Glamorgan, Wales.

Afghan Hound Society of Northern Ireland
Mr R. Margrain, Hazelbank, Cullybackey, Co. Antrim, Northern Ireland.

Afghan Hound Society of Scotland
Miss E. M. C. Holmes, Candidacasa Kennels, White Bog, Rosewell, Midlothian, Scotland.

North-Eastern Afghan Hound Society.
Mr A. Hardy, Springfield, Thorpe Road, Thorpe Threwles, Co. Durham.

THE AFGHAN STANDARD

This was adopted by the Kennel Club in 1950.

Characteristics
The Afghan Hound should be dignified and aloof with a
certain keen fierceness. The Eastern or Oriental Expression is
typical of the breed. The Afghan looks at and through one.

General appearance
The gait of the Afghan Hound should be smooth and springy
with a style of high order. The whole appearance of the dog
should give the impression of strength and dignity combining
speed and power. The head must be held proudly.

Head and skull
Skull long, not too narrow with a prominent occiput.
Foreface long, with punishing jaws and slight stop. The skull
well balanced and surmounted by a long topknot. Nose
preferably black, but liver-coloured is no fault in light-coloured
dogs.

Eyes
Should be dark for preference, but a golden colour is not
debarred. Nearly triangular, slanting slightly upwards from
the inner corner to the outer.

Ears
Should be set low and well back, carried close to the head;
covered with long silky hair.

Mouth
Level.

Neck
Long, strong, with proud carriage of the head.

Forequarters
Shoulders long and sloping, well set back, well muscled and

strong without being loaded. Forelegs straight and well boned, straight with shoulders, elbows held in.

Body

Back level, moderate length, well muscled and falling slightly away to the stern. Loin straight, broad and rather short. Hip-bones rather prominent and wide apart. A fair spring of ribs and a good depth of chest.

Hindquarters

Powerful, well bent, and well-turned stifles. Great length between hip and hock, with a comparatively short distance between hock and foot. The dew claws may be removed or allowed to remain at the discretion of the breeder.

Feet

Forefeet strong and very large, both in length and breadth, and covered with thick, long hair, toes arched, Pasterns long and springy, especially in the front, and pads well down on the ground. Hindfeet long, but not quite so broad as forefeet, covered with long thick hair.

Tail

Not too short. Set on low with ring at the end. Raised when in action. Sparsely feathered.

Coat

Long and very fine texture on ribs, fore and hindquarters and flanks. From the shoulder backward and along the saddle the hair should be short and close in mature dogs. Hair long from the forehead backward, with a distinct, silky topknot. On the foreface the hair should be short as on the back; ears and legs well coated; pasterns can be bare. The coat must be allowed to develop naturally.

Colours

All colours are acceptable.

Weight and size

Ideal height: dogs 27 to 29in. Bitches 2 to 3in. smaller.

Faults
Any appearance of coarseness. Skull too wide and foreface too short; weak underjaw. Large, round or full eyes. Neck should never be too short or thick. Back too long or too short.

7

The Borzoi

We will now deal principally with the Russian aspect of the beautiful and decorative Borzoi. Unfortunately there is no work available to them in this country and consequently a look at the scene in Britain must be restricted to the show ring.

The Borzoi, in common with so many of the large Gazehounds, was owned originally by noblemen only, but the abolition of serfdom in 1861 changed the mental outlook and social customs of the Russian people. In consequence, the social status of the Borzoi altered too.

The first mention of a Russian hunting dog appears in the middle of the thirteenth century, but the reference is to a hound that hunted hares rather than wolves, the common quarry of these dogs. Obviously from earliest times there were various breeds of hunting hounds. For instance, at one stage at the end of the last century, the Russian encyclopaedia listed eleven types. Each had a different coat and conformation, but all bore a distinct resemblance to the modern Borzoi.

Two physiques predominated. There was the shorter-haired Borzoi which was tall, and palely coloured, lemon and white or brindle and white. This was thought to be the most ancient variety and was probably nearer to the modern Greyhound than any of the other types. The other dominant breed was smaller, finer and rangier, usually dark in colour and possessing more stamina than the larger hounds. It was commonly believed that the darker-coloured animals had been outcrossed with the Crimean hound, as the dogs from that area were predominantly black with yellowish eyes and were thought to have Saluki blood. There are very early artistic records of Borzois. These exist in hunting frescoes in

Kiev's Sophia Cathedral, the fabric of which dates back to the eleventh century. These paintings show hounds of the Borzoi type chasing boars and stags, so it would seem that a curly-coated Greyhound type must have existed before the first written references.

As with so many of the Gazehounds, numbers of differing claims have been made as to their origin. Some experts state that the Borzoi was the earliest type of Greyhound and that he came south from the southern steppes of Russia with the tribes of migrants who later settled in the Orient. The dogs that remained were developed by the Russian people, but have changed very little over the centuries. Others claim that the Borzoi was the genetic result of a Greyhound — Sheepdog cross or, as already stated, a Saluki — Greyhound cross. Whatever the truth, it is indisputable that there has been a tall, curly-coated Greyhound type with a light, particoloured or dark coat in existence in Russia for many centuries.

The black-coated dogs were frowned on at one time by some of the Russian nobility. One grand duke in particular made a ruling that the dark-coloured dogs would be disqualified from hunting because their coats stood out against the snow and warned the quarry of their presence. Rumour has it that the true reason was that the duke himself preferred the paler colours and his rival's darker hounds were superior hunters. His theory on colour should not, however, be entirely discounted. In this country, poachers were always said to favour a black- or dark-coloured running dog because it couldn't be seen at night, and there is no doubt that the quarry will often spot a white dog quicker than a fawn. If one admits to the need for camouflage, the pale Borzoi would indeed be more suitable for hunting in snow.

When the liberation of the serfs caused the closure of the majority of the large estates that had worked and owned Borzois for hunting wolves and smaller game, the breed degenerated for a time. But in 1873 the Society for the Development of Hunting Dogs and Proper Conduct for Hunting was founded in Moscow. This organisation arranged dog shows and aimed to improve canine conformation and hunting capabilities.

In 1887 a supporter of the organisation, Archduke Nicolai Nikolajawitsch founded the world-famous Perchino kennels of Borzois, which he based on the best ancient Gazehound blood obtainable. Thanks to a very detailed description of this kennel written by its manager, His Excellency Dimitri Walzoff, we know the routine, hunting programmes and general layout of this magnificent organisation. The archduke himself was passionately fond of hunting and bred, as mentioned, only from the best bloodlines.

His enthusiasm bears examination. He started with sixty Borzois of varying ages and built a number of stone houses for them, each containing boxes for a dozen hounds. Every house had three paddocks and the buildings for the bitches and puppies were heated. The dogs had no heating all the year round. As is the case in many Continental kennels, the dogs were grouped, where possible, in colours. About fifty puppies were bred a year and a pack of about thirty top-quality animals were kept in a separate kennel to show to visitors.

When embarking on a wolf hunt the Duke would take about thirty-five couples with him. The couples consisted in fact of *three* hounds — two dogs and a bitch — and again they were usually selected in matching colours. The hunting field consisted of a large patch of forest running parallel to open fields. About forty riders would go ahead of the hunters and surround the territory to be hunted. If there were spaces that it was possible for a rider to cover, they would lay nets to prevent the quarry from getting away. A pack of foxhounds, also owned by the Perchino kennels, would then be sent into the forest to flush the quarry out into the fields. The Borzois were restrained on extra-long leads by riders who galloped after the wolves, then slipped the dogs that then pursued the quarry, ran level with it and bumped its flanks, while a third dog harassed from behind. Eventually the wolf would lose balance and the dogs would catch it by the ear or throat and hold on until the hunters bound up its legs and forced a wooden wedge between its teeth. The wolf hunts lasted about an hour each and the young, healthy wolves were then released into the forest again. Sometimes the Borzois were released in packs of forty or fifty after wolves, as shown in the Russian version of the film *War and Peace.*

The Perchino kennels eventually owned 130 Borzois and 15 Greyhounds and employed a staff of about 80 people. The archduke imported dogs of Russian origin from England and France to improve his stock and bought from other breeders in Russia. He bred for beauty as well as speed and kept up his interest in the Moscow shows so that he could compare types and improve on his breeding programme.

Wolf hunts on the grand Perchino scale are no longer conducted in the USSR, partly because there are few wolves in existence now, but the modern Russian Borzoi still contributes to the Russian economy. He is responsible for the success of the fur trade in that he catches foxes without mauling them. Consequently their fur is not spoilt, as it would be by shooting. The use of Borzois for this purpose is simpler than trapping, which is difficult in severe weather conditions. The dogs are also used for hare coursing, still a popular pastime in the USSR.

The Borzoi was introduced into Britain at the end of the nineteenth century by the Duchess of Newcastle, who imported the famous Perchino and his self-black-and-tan brother, Argos, who won the silver medal in Moscow in 1892. Argos was the first international Borzoi champion, for he gained his title in two countries, England and America.

Another famous import from the Perchino kennels was the all-white dog, Ooslad, who also became a champion; and Ondar, both belonging to the same kennel as the two already mentioned. The duchess's prefix was Notts and eventually she owned about a hundred dogs and became extremely famous as a breeder and a judge. Queen Alexandra's kennels at Sandringham were very well known and contributed largely to the Borzoi's popularity here. She was presented with several dogs by the Czar, Alex being the most famous, and another, Ajax, which became a champion.

At that period it was comparatively simple to import dogs from Russia, but it is almost impossible now. British stock has become somewhat interbred as a result. Although the basic British type is very similar to the Soviet animals, the Russians consider our dogs to be degenerate because they are no longer worked. The prime consideration in Russia is whether or not a dog is suitable for hunting.

The Russian State Kennels own and breed the cream of Borzoi stock. In an article in the German publication *Zehntausend und 75 Jahre Hetzhunde/Windhunde,* the writer quotes a letter received about five years ago from the Country and Economics Department of the Interior in Moscow. It reads:

> In answer to your letter, we would inform you that last year the number of Greyhound-types in the U.S.S.R. has increased. The most widely distributed breed of the Greyhound-type is the Russian long-haired Borzoi. In those States and Republics where there are large numbers of Borzois, there are, in addition to the activities of the hunters, groups of Borzoi 'friends' who encourage the general application of the breed. The dogs for breeding are the ones that have won prizes at shows, and further, possess the Ability Diploma.

The Russian standards are extremely high and they have decided theories on conformation. For example, they believe that overlong backs and overbent, very low stifles can lead to hip dysplasia. They are also immensely strict about pigmentation and all toenails must be black. There are even rules about the colour of the iris of the eye. Before a dog becomes a show champion in Russia, he must be three years old and have working certificates, as well as three of the coveted Moscow gold medals. The Russian equivalent of our challenge certificate consists of one beauty certificate and two working certificates.

Mrs Ruggles, secretary of the Borzoi Club, has visited Russia and has been to the great Moscow Show. She says the Russian Borzois are evidently very much working dogs. They are all in extremely hard condition and some are badly scarred from their working activities.

There have been only two Russian imports to Britain in the last fifty years, so its no wonder that the majority of our dogs

are frowned on by the Russians. In 1964 Sir Rudi and Lady
Sternberg were presented with a beautiful Borzoi dog, Boran.
This was a personal gift from Mr Kruschev. Sir Rudi
Sternberg was largely responsible for the British Agricultural
Show held in Moscow that year, and he and his wife gave a
very successful Sheepdog demonstration with a Border Collie
which they subsequently gave to Mr Kruschev. He, in turn,
was so delighted that Boran was produced to show his
gratitude. Boran was the winner of two gold medallions and
arrived in this country complete with his working and show
medals. By all accounts he was a great character. In the six
years he spent in Britain before his death, he never reacted to
any word of English, but would obey any instructions given
him in Russian without hesitation. To have amassed so many
medals in Russia is no easy feat.

The Russian working trials, particularly, are judged severely
by three judges on horses, one of whom must be chosen by
the fur industry. The dogs are coursed after hares or foxes.
Show judging is similar to the Continental method where
dogs are graded, excellent, very good, good and so on down
the scale, and are grouped in three sections, ranging from
ten-month-old puppies to dogs of three years and more.
Boran, as a gold-medal winner, naturally had the grading
excellent.

A number of British-bred dogs have Boran behind them,
in particular those belonging to Miss Murray of the Fortrouge
prefix and Mr J. Bennett-Heard, husband of the late Mrs
Jackie Bennett-Heard who died early in 1974. She was a great
believer both in Russian ethics and in keeping the Russian
blood which, she felt, mixed well with English bloodlines.
Boran produced five champions in only three litters. Three of
these were bred by Miss Murray, namely Ch. Zircon and Ch.
Zest of Fortrouge — they are still in her ownership, and Ch.
Matalona Sudorka of Fortrouge, now owned by Mrs Ruggles.
The remaining two champions came from Mrs Bennett-
Heard's kennel and were out of her bitch, Ch. Angelola of
Enolam, who was one of the top-winning show-ring bitches
for 1963 and 1967 and was bred by Mrs Malone. These were
Ch. Keepers Kwango and Ch. Keepers the Baron. The latter

was the top stud dog for 1973 and he himself sired six champions. One of these, Ch. Keepers the Baroness, has won ten challenge certificates.

Mrs Bennett-Heard imported a young dog, Keroj of Keepers, from Russia at the end of 1972. He should produce a great opportunity for British breeders interested in regaining the Russian bloodlines. It is greatly to his late owner's credit that she managed to bring him to this country despite the many difficulties involved.

As stated at the beginning of this chapter, the Borzoi has had no work provided for him in Britain. Efforts have been made to course him, but the attempts were not successful as many show owners are afraid of injuring top-quality stock. Nevertheless, the basic instinct to chase wolves must still influence the behaviour of these hounds. Ch. Keepers Kwango leapt to the defence of a kennel maid who had been attacked by two Alsatians while exercising a Borzoi bitch at the Keepers kennel. Kwango pinned one Alsatian to the ground, tore the throat of the other, and caused multiple injuries to both. As a result of this intervention, the kennel girl and the Borzoi bitch were rescued without fatal injuries. This demonstrates admirably the courage of the breed.

Unfortunately Borzois are not coursed or raced seriously in Britain. Steps were taken to race them by the late Mr and Mrs Edgar Sayer, who bred Greyhounds and Borzois which they used to trial on their own track; other owners were invited to do the same. Since their death no further attempts have been made to race them.

For the present anyway, the Borzoi must therefore be restricted to the show ring in Britain. The registration figures at the Kennel Club hover somewhere between the Irish Wolfhound and the Saluki and, like the other hound breeds, they continue to rise.

There are many hunting stories about Borzois, but the most fascinating one is of historic rather than sporting interest. It concerns Milka, the Borzoi bitch belonging to the last of the Russian czars. She was a large, almost black, hound and, since the future of the Russian people depended on the fate of the czarevitch she was a much respected and admired animal. The monk Rasputin was her only enemy, her animal instinct leading her to believe he was an evil influence on her master. Whenever he approached the Czarevitch's bedside, Milka growled and curled her lip at him.

Eventually, Milka bit Rasputin on the cheek when he leant over the bed of the sick Czarevitch. As a result the Czarina was persuaded to remove Milka permanently from her son's bedroom. Prince Orloff and the remainder of the royal family, all enemies of Rasputin, were outraged and the Czarevitch himself was heartbroken. Nevertheless his mother's faith in Rasputin prevailed and the Borzoi was made to sleep outside the bedroom door rather than at the bedside.

Plans were made by the royal family to assassinate Rasputin, but none of them were put into effect at that stage. Early one morning, a palace servant was heard shrieking with fear as he ran down the echoing hall from the Czarevich's bedroom. He had found Milka dead in a pool of blood with her throat cut outside her master's room. It was never discovered if Rasputin or an accomplice killed her, but the fury aroused by her death and the determination, from then on, of the Orloffs to rid themselves of Rasputin and his evil influence on the royal family was a cause of the Russian Revolution.

It's so easy to forget a breed's origins and this is the reason for concluding the chapter at this point. It is vital that the characteristics and breed history from the country of origin of any breed should not be lost and it is to be hoped that Russia will release more stock to provide new bloodlines in other parts of the world.

The secretary of the Borzoi Club is: Mrs Eileen Ruggles, Maldon Hall, Spital Road, Maldon, Essex.

THE BORZOI STANDARD

Adopted in 1922.

Characteristics
Alertness, dignity and courage.

General appearance
Very graceful, aristocratic and elegant, combining courage, muscular power and great speed.

Head and skull
Head long and lean; well filled in below the eyes; measurement equal from the occiput to the inner corner of the eye, and from the inner corner of the eye to the tip of the nose. Skull very slightly domed and narrow, stop not perceptible, inclining to a Roman nose. Head fine so that the direction of the bones and principal veins can be clearly seen. Bitches' heads should be finer than dogs'. Jaws long, deep and powerful; nose large and black, not pink or brown, nicely rounded, neither cornered nor sharp. Viewed from above should look narrow, converging very gradually to the tip of the nose.

Eyes
Dark, intelligent, alert and keen. Almond-shaped, set obliquely, placed well back, but not too far apart. Eye rims dark. Eyes should not be light, round or staring.

Ears
Small and fine in quality; not too far apart. They should be active and responsive; when alert can be erect; when in repose nearly touching at the occiput.

Mouth
Teeth even, neither pig-jawed nor undershot.

Neck
Clean, slightly arched; reasonably long; powerful. Well set on and free from throatiness. Flat at the sides, not round.

Forequarters
Shoulders clean, sloping well back, fine at withers, free from lumpiness. Forelegs lean and straight. Seen from the front, narrow-like blades; from the side, wide at shoulder, narrowing down to foot; elbows neither turned in nor out; pasterns strong flexible and springy.

Body
Chest, great depth of brisket, rather narrow. Ribs well sprung
and flexible; neither flat-sided nor barrel-shaped. Very deep,
giving heart room and lung play, especially in the case of
mature males [it is from depth of chest rather than breadth
that the Borzoi derives its heart room and lung play]. Back
rising in a graceful arch from as near the shoulder as possible
with a well-balanced fall-away. The arch to be more marked
in dogs than bitches. Rather boney, muscular and free from
any cavity. Muscles highly developed and well distributed.

Hindquarters
Loins broad and very powerful, with plenty of muscular
development. Quarters should be wider than shoulders,
ensuring stability of stance. Thighs long, well developed with
good second thigh. Hindlegs long, muscular, stifles well bent,
hocks broad, clean and well let down.

Feet
Front feet rather long, toes close together; well arched, never
flat, neither turning in nor out. Hindfeet hare-like, i.e.
longer and less arched.

Tail
Long, rather low set. Well feathered, carried low, not gaily.
In action may be used as a rudder, but not rising above the
level of the back. From hocks may be sickle-shaped, but not
ringed.

Coat
Long and silky (never woolly) either flat or wavy or rather
curly. Short and smooth on head, ears and front of legs, on
neck the frill profuse and rather curly, forelegs and chest well
feathered on hindquarters and tail feathering long and
profuse.

Colour
Immaterial. In the opinion of the club a dog should never be
penalised for being self-coloured.

Size
Height at shoulders: dogs from 29in. upwards; bitches from 27in. upwards.

Faults
Short neck, coarse and big ears. 'Dish-faced', coarse head, light or round eyes; straight shoulders, flat back, arch starting too far back, too narrow in front. Round bone, straight hocks, weak quarters, coarse coat, splay-footed, too close behind, also lack of quality and lack of condition.

8

The Deerhound

There are many conflicting theories on the background of the Deerhound. It is believed that he was brought to Scotland by the Celts and is a descendant of either the Highland Greyhound, or the Scottish Greyhound, or even the huge Irish Wolf dog. Most evidence points to the fact that the latter was smooth-coated until the breed was revived at the end of the last century by Captain Graham, so the two previous ideas are most probably correct. The Highland Greyhound was heavier in build than the Scottish Greyhound, but both were reported as having rough coats by Pennant in 1769 and William Youatt in his *The Dog*, published early in the nineteenth century. Descriptions of ears and other characteristics varied, so no doubt numbers of both breeds were outcrossed to other types of hunting hound.

The modern Deerhound is tall, but not as bulky as the Irish Wolfhound, and achieves working qualities along with great elegance. Unlike the majority of Gazehounds he is more restricted in colour. He should be self-coloured, and a bluey-grey is the most popular shade, with only very minor white points allowed. Anything so obvious as a white collar or blaze is penalised in the show ring. With the exception of the Irish Wolfhound and the Pharaoh Hound, all types of colour variations are common in other Gazehound breeds.

The gipsies for many years have called a Deerhound/ Lurcher a Stag cross. Their ideas on the history of the term vary. I suspect it originates from the dog's function in life. Also he is very near in appearance to the old illustrations of Staghounds — not, it should be noted the modern Staghound. In the Middle Ages hunting hounds were crossed with Greyhounds for extra speed, but a large, often rough-

Mrs. Nagle's Champion Sulhamstead Match at exercise; *below*, Mrs. Florence Nagle at Cruft's 1960 with her Irish Wolfhound Sulhamstead Merman, who was best in show

An Irish Wolfhound puppy. It is necessary to have such bone and bulk at this early age; *below*, a Greyhound/Bedlington cross Lurcher at speed

Above, an adult Pharaoh Hound. Behind her there is a reproduction from the tomb of Antefa 11 (3,000 B.C.), showing a hound from which the breed is thought to be derived; *below*, Pharaoh Hound puppies

Above, a Saluki gives an admirable demonstration of the beauty of the Gazehound in repose; *below*, a pair of Miss Watkin's Windswift Salukis

coated Greyhound was frequently used for stags. Colonel Hamilton Smith's illustration of a Staghound reprinted in Phyllis Gardner's *The Irish Wolfhound* shows a head very similar to the modern Deerhound. In the Prado Museum in Madrid there are two paintings by Paul de Vos of large, Greyhound types, some with smooth and others with rough hair, pulling down a stag. These were painted in the seventeenth century. The Brussels tapestry entitled 'Triumph of the Goddess Diana' in the Rijksmuseum, Amsterdam, also shows rough-haired Greyhounds with dead game, including deer. It is an early eighteenth-century work.

The gipsies prefer the Stag or Deerhound-cross to almost any other, and this speaks well for the working capabilities of these hounds. No poacher will gladly suffer a dog incapable of providing his supper, and the Deerhound's rough coat does not tear in thick cover as would the Greyhound's finer skin. Originally the Deerhound was used for tracking the deer and holding it at bay, often in very perilous conditions, until the forester came to dispatch it. Coursing, too, was popular until superseded by the rifle and stalking.

There were two methods commonly employed: the most conventional course involved a small group of enthusiasts who stalked a deer until it broke cover. The hounds would then be slipped. Occasionally three or four were used. The quarry was eventually killed by the force of the dog's leap as he caught and held the deer by the ear, the foreleg or the throat. Both the dogs and their quarry were running at peak speeds at that stage. The deer was pulled down and his neck usually broken by the weight of the dog at his head.

Another popular method was to drive the deer in large numbers towards the waiting hunters who lay with their dogs in hiding. The deer would have been herded towards the hunting ground several days beforehand so that they were readily available on the day of the hunt. An event of this sort is described in 'Lays of the Deerforest' and was arranged for the entertainment of Mary, Queen of Scots, in 1563 by the Earl of Athol.

The strength of the Deerhound is confirmed in many

coursing stories. It takes a powerful animal to hold a Stag at bay, for the latter frequently rushes to water when pursued. The dogs then have to hold him on a slippery surface in strong currents and waterfalls. Consequently, many Scottish legends have sprung up round these dogs and one of the best is told in Mr J. Wentworth Day's *The Dog in Sport*. Here it is:

> Pentland Moor if your hounds hold her, and your head is off if they lose her — was the ultimatum of the Bruce to Sir William St. Clair. They were hunting deer on Pentland Moor. Sir William boasted that his two hounds, Help and Hold, would take any stag roused. And as would happen on such a day they roused the magic white deer, the deer that no living hound might hold.
>
> Off went the deer, the hounds in hot pursuit, the King blazing with excitement, Sir William, we may assume, slightly sick with apprehension. It was not the sort of bet that a medieval Ladbroke could afford to smile at. The stag reached the edge of March Burn, plunged in, swam strongly for the other side. Had he reached it Sir William's head would have been off. But Help and Hold plunged into the Burn, followed the stag, bayed it and held it. Up came the forester with his knife — and the white stag's day was done, Sir William's head safe, and the whole of Pentland Moor his own.

When stalking began, the working days of the Deerhound declined — despite their use for tracking. By the beginning of the nineteenth century their numbers had seriously decreased. One writer of the period states that there were probably only about a dozen in Scotland, but Mr McNeill of Colonsay and his brother, Lord Colonsay, gave the breed a tremendous boost by breeding and rearing the best dogs from the working stock available. By the middle of the century numbers had risen and they were readily available in the Highlands. A further setback followed, but a group of breeders in the South of England helped to bring about another upsurge in the breed.

At the end of the last century, Stonehenge in his *British Dogs of the Islands* (published in 1882) classifies the Deerhound as a Retriever and says:

This dog is now more ornamental than useful, his former trade of retrieving wounded deer in Scotland being often entrusted to Colleys [*sic*] whole or half-bred, and cross-bred dogs of various kinds, but in the south his grand size and outline make him a great favourite with country gentlemen and more especially with the ladies of the families . . .

This was a reference in part to the recent and first appearance of the Deerhound in the show ring. The first man to show these dogs was Colonel Inge, who entered two at Birmingham in 1859. From then on the Deerhound was frequently exhibited. The greatest bitch winner ever, was bred by Mr Harry Rawson of the St Ronan's prefix. She was called St Ronan's Rhyme and was born in 1902. She won the Kennel Club cup for the champion of champions in 1906 and 1907 and in the same two years the Scottish Kennel Club champion-of-show cup. Another kennel with a tremendous influence on all show stock, even up to the present day, was the Ross kennel, founded by the Misses Loughrey, that produced the very famous sire, Ch. Tragic of Ross. He was the grandsire of Ch. Freda of Enterkine — owned and bred by Miss Bell.

The current top kennels are many, but the most successful dual-purpose one is undoubtedly Miss Anastasia Noble's. She herself is from the Western Highlands and has bred two of the breed's most famous champions, Tessa and Monarch of Ardkinglas. Another famous bitch from this kennel, Ch. Aurora of Ardkinglas, has twice been best in show, all breeds, at champion shows, and is the dam of five champions in only two litters. She is also the winner of the Dava Quaich coursing trophy. So the breed is once more well established in Scotland. Miss Noble is chairman of the Deerhound Club, and in recent years has again provided these hounds with sport and entertainment by introducing them to hare coursing. This has been extremely successful and her stock has won the Ardkinglas Coursing Trophy for the most points gained during the season for three years running. The following is her own description of how the Deerhound has adapted to this sport:

"Deerhounds, as their name implies, are intended to hunt deer, originally for the pot and later for sport. The breed has changed little for many years, judging from descriptions and pictures. The earliest painting I know personally is by Fernley, the late eighteenth-century artist. It shows hounds, exactly like many today, although not so hairy as some. I am not sure when the heavier coats came in, but I fancy that, with regular work, they would tend to come off anyway.

"There was a period when Deerhounds were used in conjunction with rifles. The hounds would track the wounded beasts. All sorts of crosses were tried at that time, hence the very odd-looking animals seen in pictures of that period. I refer to the last part of the nineteenth century approximately. However, some pure-bred strains were always maintained and when, finally, the Kennel Club was founded and shows began, a number of people registered their hounds and showed them. As a result, there was a nucleus of people who kept the breed going as field work declined. However much some working owners deride the show-ring cult and animals bred for it, I am convinced that without it our breed would have died out. As it is, we have a very small stock from which to breed, and no pure outcross available in the breed anywhere in the world. All stock stems from the few in this country. This is a tricky situation and I think new blood will need to be introduced again.

"Deerhounds' real work in this country is virtually dead. Facilities and terrain are difficult to obtain, but the instinct to work is still there and when the hounds have the chance of running deer they do so. I believe that chasing a moving animal is very basic to all dogs and more so, of course, in sighthounds, so the instinct is not easily lost, even if the refinements are sometimes lacking.

"In the early 1950s one of our members, Kenneth Cassels, had the idea of organising coursing meetings for Deerhounds, both at deer and hares in Scotland. This he succeeded in doing and all working-hound enthusiasts should be very grateful to him for the initiative he showed and the keenness he engendered in most owners, which made the coursing the success it is.

"The first meeting was in 1954 and meetings on Dava Moor in Morayshire have continued ever since. At first they were private meetings run by Mr Cassels, but later he handed over to the Saluki Club that had a good coursing organisation going and agreed to include Deerhounds. So for many years now that meeting has been run jointly with a lot of friendly rivalry and jokes. It is the senior event for Deerhounds, although Salukis and Wolfhounds had occasional meetings before the last war. It is also the best for our hounds as they are in their natural surroundings. It is lovely to see them, first keyed up and alert, and then going full stretch over the moor. It would be better maybe if they were after deer, but blue hares are a good substitute.

"Deerhound coursing is not as fast as Greyhound coursing, and work, in the way of turning, is much less. Judging has to be slightly modified so that decisions can be made without too many 'no courses'. Even in these, hounds may run a long way so that they become exhausted and, as a result, run out of hares and time. Deerhounds do not run with absolute speed and fury. They look where they are going and are stayers rather than sprinters. Consequently, one needs much larger areas to course over and these are not easy to come by for both an obliging landowner and a reasonable supply of the essential 'raw material' — hares — are needed.

"Apart from Morayshire our other main meetings are in Lincolnshire and Norfolk, mostly on fenland over which the dogs run very long courses. We are very grateful to all the landowners who lend us ground and do their utmost to help us.

"Deerhounds will often course for very long distances and some, after running awhile, will suddenly change into top gear and forge ahead. Their size is a disadvantage for turning and picking up the hare, but they manage. Sometimes the comparatively slow-looking large ones are eating up the ground with their long stride and leaving smaller, more agile dogs behind. People argue always about the best type for coursing, but in my opinion the really important factor is intelligence and determination. If they have the will to go, they will get over all physical problems within reason. The hounds with this attribute are a real joy to see and handle.

"It is not easy to say that any strain is really better than another, particularly as Deerhounds are all very closely related. Many have never been tried, either because their owners are not keen or because they have not the time to attend meetings. On the whole my own Ardkinglas, Miss Bell's Enterkine and Mrs Young's Portsonachan hounds have done best over the years because we have been the keenest and most consistent supporters among the breeders, and working enthusiasts have bought stock from us.

"Many hounds that come to our meetings are complete novices. Some are scared of slips and difficult to get sighted, but usually they come to it well. The experienced ones make a dash for the slipper if near him and once in slips are a joy to watch. On the whole a rather shorter slip is needed for they are slower on the run and, if given too much law, or start and a strong hare, only a chase will ensue. This makes it quite difficult for the slipper to make his decision. A hare running at right angles is often good, for it gives the hounds a good sight and, because the dogs are slow turning, the hare still has plenty of law.

"All our meetings are walked up — we cannot afford beaters — although we sometimes have small drives with volunteers. Consequently, it is advisable to get oneself as fit as one's hound. Hounds should be in as hard a condition as is possible, otherwise they cannot be expected to give of their best. If they are really keen they could easily do themselves harm. The less keen will merely stop when tired. Even the keenest will do so at times when feeling out of sorts, as bitches frequently do when only two or three months out of season. For this reason I think it is not dangerous to run them at that time, merely disappointing.

"To get hounds fit does not necessarily involve miles of road work, although they can take it, of course, if you have the time and energy. A regular distance of about two to four miles a day for about a month before a meeting is ideal, depending on how unfit your hound is before the season starts. Just slogging along a road is dull, and dogs should have some free galloping, if possible, over rough and/or hilly ground, as this develops the muscles and encourages them to look after themselves. It also helps their mental development. Road work has always been considered the best way of keeping fit and, as trainers over the years cannot all be wrong, it is obviously good, but one need not feel it essential to do vast distances. Bicycles and horses provide a better speed for accompanying hounds than walking. I am against exercising with a car as one tends to go faster than one thinks — and one does not have the same contact with one's hound.

"It takes experience to assess your dog's fitness and all hounds vary. The art is to get them to peak fitness for the right day. Feed them as well as possible and starve them the night before running, or just give them a snack meal. This can be difficult if it is a two- or three-day meeting. However, I believe starving, or nearly so, is preferable to feeding anything amounting to a normal-sized meal. Many people have their own theories on foods to help their hounds and many old and weird tips are given in Greyhound books. Personally, I favour honey, eggs and milk as a combination. Just a little should be given in the morning or very late the night before coursing. Try to give your hound the best possible preparation and chance for running, then hope for the best on the day. Luck is needed too in this sport.

"Hare coursing may not be the Deerhound's true work, but it gives him some sport and keeps the working instinct alive. It has also given Deerhound owners a great deal of pleasure and amusement, both in the field and socially at coursing gatherings.

"In conclusion I should like to say that we are most grateful to the Greyhound people and their slippers and judges for all the support and encouragement they have given us, particularly Gordon Brooks, who has been an immense help, and the slipper David Green, who has given a Trophy for one of our stakes."

The current show winners are many, but Miss A. N.
Hartley's Rotherwood prefix must be one of the most famous.
Her bitch, Ch. Fulvia of Rotherwood was the top winning
bitch for 1973 and she has bred such well-known hounds as
Ch. Francisca of Rotherwood, one of the most successful
bitches in 1966, and Ch. Garry of Rotherwood, the top dog
in 1965. She is also the secretary of the Deerhound Club and
the author of a most interesting book on these hounds.

Another famous breeder, Miss Linton of the Geltsdale
prefix, bred Ch. Brandt of Geltsdale, who, with Miss M.
Bell's Ch. Laurie of Enterkine, shared the greatest number of
dog challenge certificates during 1967. Both the Geltsdale
and Enterkine kennels are long established as are Dr Poyner
Wall's Melchior prefix and Mrs Dickinson's Champflower
kennels. There are numbers of other top winners who deserve
mention. Among these are Miss Edwards's Ch. Manshay
Alaric of Tarffa, who has nineteen challenge certificates and
the same owner's Ch. Shona of Tarff. During 1975 Miss
Linton's Ch. Geltsdale Torquil was highly successful as was
Miss Cox's Dufault kennel. No less than three dogs from here
gained their championship titles that year.

At present the breed is well supported without having
reached a dangerous level of popularity. The breeders rear
and choose their bloodlines with immense care and, as field
work is now provided, there would seem to be little danger of
degeneration of the Deerhound.

The secretary of the Deerhound Club is: Miss A. N.
Hartley, Fletton Tower, Peterborough, PE2 9AB.

THE DEERHOUND STANDARD

Head and skull
The head should be broadest at the ears, tapering slightly to
the eyes, with the muzzle tapering more decidedly to the
nose. The muzzle should be pointed but lips level. The head
should be long, the skull rather flat than round, with a very
slight rise over the eyes, but with nothing approaching a stop.
The skull should be coated with moderately long hair, which
is softer than the rest of the coat. The nose should be black

(though in some blue-fawns the colour is blue) and slightly aquiline. In the lighter-coloured dogs a black muzzle is preferred. There should be a good moustache of rather silky hair, and a fair beard.

Eyes
The eyes should be dark — generally they are dark brown or hazel. A very light eye is not liked. The eye is moderately full, with a soft look in repose, but a keen, faraway look when the dog is roused. The rims of the eyelids should be black.

Ears
The ears should be set on high, and, in repose, folded back like the Greyhound's, though raised above the head in excitement without losing the fold, and even in some cases semi-erect. A prick ear is bad. A big, thick ear hanging flat to the head, or heavily coated with long hair, is the worst of faults. The ear should be soft, glossy, and like a mouse's coat to the touch, and the smaller it is the better. It should have no long coat, or long fringe, but there is often a silky, silvery coat on the body of the ear and the tip. Whatever the general colour, the ears should be black or dark in colour.

Mouth
Teeth level.

Neck
The neck should be long; that is, of the length that benefits the Greyhound character of the dog. An over-long neck is not necessary or desirable, for the dog is not required to stoop to his work like a Greyhound, and it must be remembered that the mane, which every good specimen should have, detracts from the apparent length of neck. The nape of the neck should be very prominent where the head is set on, and the throat should be clean-cut at the angle and prominent. Moreover, a Deerhound requires a very strong neck to hold a stag.

Forequarters
The shoulders should be well sloped, the blades well back and not too much width between them. Loaded and straight shoulders are very bad faults. The forelegs should be straight, broad and flat, a good broad forearm and elbow being desirable.

Body
The body and general formation is that of a Greyhound of larger size and bone. Chest deep rather than broad, but not too narrow and flat-sided. The loin well arched and drooping to the tail. A straight back is not desirable, this formation being unsuitable for going uphill and very unsightly.

Hindquarters
Drooping, and as broad and as powerful as possible; the hips being set wide apart. The hindlegs should be well bent at the stifle, with great length from the hip to the hock, which should be broad and flat.

Feet
Should be close and compact, with well-arranged toes; nails strong.

Tail
Should be long, thick at the root, tapering and reaching to about 1½in. off the ground. When the dog is still, dropped perfectly straight down, or curved. When in motion it should be curved; when excited, in no case to be lifted out of the line of the back. It should be well covered with hair; on the inside, thick and wiry; on the underside, longer and towards the end a slight fringe is not objectionable. A curl or ring tail is most undesirable.

Coat
The hair on the body, neck and quarters should be harsh and wiry, and about 3 or 4in. long; that on the head, breast and belly is much softer. There should be a slightly hairy fringe on the inside of the fore- and hindlegs, but nothing

approaching the 'feather' of a Collie. The Deerhound should be a shaggy dog, but not over-coated. A woolly coat is bad. Some good strains have a mixture of silky coat with the hard, which is preferable to a woolly coat; but the proper coat is a thick, close-lying one, ragged, and harsh or crisp to the touch.

Colour
Colour is much a matter of fancy. But there is no manner of doubt that the dark-blue-grey is the most preferred because quality tends to follow this colour. Next come the darker and lighter greys or brindles, the darkest being generally preferred. Yellow and sandy-red or red-fawn, especially with black points, i.e., ears and muzzles, are also in equal estimation, this being the colour of the oldest known strains, the McNeil and Chesthill Menzies. White is condemned by all the old authorities, but a white chest and white toes, occurring as they do in a great many of the darkest-coloured dogs, are not so greatly objected to, but the less the better, as the Deerhound is a self-coloured dog. A white blaze on the head, or a white collar should be heavily penalised. In other cases, though passable, an attempt should be made to get rid of white markings. The less white the better, but a slight white tip to the stern occurs in the best strains.

Weight and size
Weight should be 85 - 105lb in dogs and 65 - 80lb in bitches. The height of dogs should not be less than 30in. and of bitches 28in., at the shoulder.

Faults
Thick ears hanging flat to the head, or heavily coated with long hair. Curl or ring tail. Light eye; straight back; cow hocks, weak pasterns, straight stifles, splay feet, woolly coat; loaded and straight shoulders; white markings.

9

The Greyhound

Historically, the Greyhound is the most important of the entire Gazehound group. Not only do all Gazehounds descend from the Greyhound/Saluki type, but the Greyhound as a specific breed has developed numerically and physically to a very great extent over the last seventy years. Three distinct sections — for the British Greyhound only — now exist, devoted respectively to racing, coursing and show dogs.

The Greyhound came to Britain with the Celts in the fourth century *BC*. Recent evidence has shown that he may have arrived in Cornwall even earlier with the Phoenicians, who exchanged dogs for the local minerals. Similar transactions were conducted in Europe by the Greeks a little later, so that varying types of Greyhound were eventually to be found throughout the Continent.

From the first they were used in Britain for rabbiting, whether they were rough- or smooth-coated, or with rose-shaped or flying ears. From the eleventh to the fifteenth centuries they were exclusively the nobleman's coursing dog. The forest laws forbade any lowlier sportsman to own a running dog for fear of spoiling the pastime of royalty. By the time of Elizabeth I, hawking and coursing were aristocratic obsessions. This is evident in Shakespeare's plays, particularly *The Taming of the Shrew,* in which there are constant references to both sports.

It seems probable that the smooth-coated, rose-eared variety of dog was the most popular. This can be judged by such paintings as Ucello's 'Hunt in a Forest' at the Ashmolean Museum, Oxford, Pisanello's 'Vision of St Eustace' at the National Gallery and Beeldemaeker's 'The Hunter' at the Rijksmuseum in Amsterdam — to name just three. There are any number of paintings showing rough- and smooth-coated types, all varying in size, but the large, smooth-coated type predominates and it is not very different from the modern coursing Greyhound. These dogs were used as a valuable out-cross to the heavier, hunting hounds, such as the Southern Hound and the Talbot, to produce a racier outline and the increase in speed that one associates with the modern Foxhound.

When, at the end of the last century, the Greyhound ceased to be simply a coursing hound and his owners turned to the track and the show ring for further entertainment, the vast changes within the breed itself began to come about. The difference between racing and coursing dogs is not marked, but the show animal has become separated genetically and in appearance from the other two groups. The first show Greyhounds came from coursing stock — because there was no other — and consequently they were working dogs. The judges were specialists who used their hounds for sporting purposes. Gradually as the show enthusiasts began to breed from only the best-looking coursing dogs, so the variation in type began to develop. A great deal of show stock originated in Cornwall, so show dogs became known as Cornish Greyhounds. The advent of the all-rounder judge (chosen by the canine societies because he could cover several breeds at one show, thereby benefitting them financially) did nothing to save the situation. These judges frequently had no interest in preserving the working qualities of a hound, if in fact they even recognised a coursing Greyhound when they saw one!

The essential differences that have now emerged between the three types are interesting. The coursing dog is smaller, shorter-coupled and more barrel-chested than the racing or show dog. The racing Greyhound is very variable in conformation and size. For example, a racing bitch can be any weight from 50 to 70lb, and a dog anything from 60 to 80lb. The chief goal of racing breeders is obviously speed, so the breeding often does not follow a pattern, and consequently it is almost impossible to guess the result of a mating beforehand.

Show dogs, on the other hand, are much more even in

type; a bitch can vary from 60 to 70lb and a dog from 70 to 80lb. Racing dogs have tremendously powerful, wide chests, with huge bulky shoulders, and strong, heavy necks. The show Greyhounds are much more elegant with fine, flat, oblique shoulders, and sometimes a tendency to kipper sides. They are taller and their hindquarters are narrower, with a much more pronounced bend of stifle than the average racing dog has.

The beauty of the Greyhound is unquestionable, but only a few coursing or racing dogs can match their show brethren. The former tend towards coarseness and an over-muscling that would eliminate them in the show ring. Unlike his smaller counterpart, the Whippet, the Greyhound undoubtedly coarsens when trained strenuously for either coursing or racing.

Both sports are run by professionals and are highly competitive. Training is time-absorbing and neither owners nor trainers can easily participate in more than one occupation.

As a result of the split in the breed, there are two stud books for Greyhounds: one for those registered with the National Coursing Club and the other for the Kennel Club-registered show dogs. When a litter of coursing or racing Greyhounds is born, the puppies must be registered with the National Coursing Club within two months of their date of birth. On the other hand, application for registration to the Kennel Club can be made for show dogs at any age, although, at the time of writing, an entirely new system of registration for show dogs is planned.

The difference in figures between the two clubs is considerable. In *The Review of Coursing,* mentioned previously, the authors give a table of records from 1883 from the National Coursing Club Greyhound Stud Book. This is worked out in five-yearly cycles. In 1965, for example, 3,489 dogs were registered and in 1970 the figure was 3,872, while in 1934 the number was as high as 9,300. The Kennel Club registrations (given in the same publication from the year 1945) totalled a mere 30 in 1965 and 85 in 1970, the highest figure up to that year being 145 in 1947. More recent calculations put the figures for the last two years at approximately 5,000 registrations with the National Coursing Club and about a hundred with the Kennel Club.

In the last ten years there has been an attempt at a rapprochement between show and working dogs. The Greyhound Club managed to arrange for show classes to be put on for racing or coursing dogs and these have usually been better supported than others. At the West of England Ladies Kennel Society Show of 1973, for example, there were eight exhibits in the working-dog class and the post-graduate bitch class was the only other to have as many entries.

Mrs Elizabeth Richardson, who lives in Hampshire and breeds and rears racing Greyhounds, believes that there is a greater chance of a good, working Greyhound being placed in the show ring than a show dog achieving success on the track. This is partly the result of the greater numbers bred for working purposes, among which there must be some good-lookers, if only on the laws of average. She claims, too, that a racing litter looks completely different from a show-bred one, and that the fronts on racing puppies are stronger and wider from a very early age. She is the first person to have shown a racing Greyhound at Cruft's for thirteen years and won the novice class there in 1969 with her brindle dog Melody Max. The famous Endless Gossip, which set a record time for his day of 28.50sec. in the 1952 Greyhound Derby, also won a first at Cruft's in 1956, when he was handled by Mrs Idella Smith, a well-known judge of Greyhounds and Whippets. She herself was the owner of the show-bred dog Beau Sabreur of Loven, who raced at Catford and Wimbledon and held two track records. He too was a Cruft's winner.

Further problems can arise when combining track and show activities. Mrs Richardson points out that, when training Melody Max for show from about nine months of age, he became accustomed to holding his head high in the ring, with the result that when he started his racing he continued to hold his head high on the track. At present she is showing a son of Max, but he too has just commenced racing training and she feels it is wrong to upset his track routine with

constant showing. As a result, he will not be shown until he
retires from the track. This is one of the few kennels that
shows racing dogs, but the problems are obviously considerable. Strangely enough, in Ireland the show classes are full of
racing dogs, but there are exceptionally few kennels there for
show dogs.

Of the well-known racing dogs that are sufficiently
beautiful to be shown, Mrs Richardson mentions the famous
stud dog, Camira Story, and Mr Edwards-Clarke, in his book
The Popular Greyhound, cites the coursing dog, Dee Rock,
as an example of classic conformation.

The show ring is undoubtedly dominated at the moment by
Mrs John Wilton-Clark's very successful Shalfleet kennel. Her
litter brother and sister, the brindle Ch. Shalfleet Sir
Lancelot, and the blue Ch. Shalfleet Spode, were the top
winners for 1972 and 1973. Spode is the first blue in the
breed to gain her championship title. Sir Lancelot was best in
show at the Hound Association Championship Show in 1972
and reserve best in show there in 1973. To add to this, he
won the Hound group at Cruft's in 1973.

The most successful Greyhound win at Cruft's was achieved
by Mrs Judy de Casembroot's Ch. Treetops Golden Falcon,
who was best in show in 1956. The same kennel produced Ch.
Treetops Hawk, sire of thirty champions — a breed record.
Another post-war kennel was the Seagift establishment owned
by Mrs Dorothy Whitwell, who had seventeen of the forty-five
champions made up between 1948 and 1964. Mrs Whitwell
no longer shows Greyhounds, but judges a number of
breeds.

One must also mention such famous show dogs as Mrs Eve
Young and Miss Pamela Vogel's Ch. Playgirl Tammy, the top
winning bitch from 1966 to 1969 inclusive. Mrs Young's later
acquisition, Ch. Wenonah Goosander, is also highly successful
and has group and best in show wins to her credit. Mr Frank
Brown's Shaunvalley prefix is behind Ch. Shaunvalley Mudlark
and Ch. Shaunvalley Cavalier, both top winners in the late
1960s.

Yet another well-known kennel in Egloshayle Cornwall is
owned by Mrs Ralph Parsons who has bred many a good one,

each with the initials R.P., including her present successful dog Rosyer Poner, and a foundation dog from Mrs Michael Gwynn's Starbolt kennel, Ch. Starbolt Roll on Pay Day. The latter kennel produced the best-of-breed winner at Cruft's 1974, Ch. Starbolt Cetus.

When considering working dogs, there are here again so many good ones it's difficult to know which to pinpoint. Master McGrath, Cerito and Coomassie, however, all won the Waterloo Cup three times and Fullerton four times in 1889, 1890, 1891 and 1892 (the 1889 win was divided with his kennel companion Trough End). Dee Rock, previously mentioned, sired three winners of four Waterloo Cups: Delightful Devon in 1939, De Flint in 1940 and Swinging Light in 1941 and 1942. The black, Red Robin, sire of Swinging Light, was another successful stud dog and he in turn was produced by Staff Officer, who sired four Waterloo Cup winners in all. In recent years, Best Champagne (sire of Just Better, winner of the Waterloo Cup in 1966) and Haich Bee are both siring good stock and are certainly among the most successful of modern sires.

One must not forget the really noteworthy coursing wins that have come about since 1960. Here I must mention Mr Thomas Ahern's Celbridge Chance, who won the Irish Cup twice — in 1960 and 1961 — as did Spring Twilight in 1964 and 1966. In 1965 Nicely Ahead not only won the Waterloo Cup, but also went on to win the Purse the following year. In 1971, Lord Sefton's So Clever, sired by the well-known stud, How Clever, won the Cup. This was the Sefton family's first Waterloo Cup win since 1921, although their dogs have been runners-up on six or seven occasions. Lord Sefton had been trying to win it ever since his father's triumph in the 1920s, and his dog achieved this just in time, for his owner died the following year.

In 1943 the puppy Countryman won the Cup. Other puppies to have won since are Maesydd Michael in 1947, Rodney Magnet in 1970, and Linden Eland in 1972.

In the racing world, as already mentioned, a new record was set in 1973 by Patricia's Hope who won the Greyhound Derby for the second year running in 28.68sec. He was trained by John O'Connor in County Cork and is the first Greyhound to win the Derby twice since Mick the Miller did so in 1929 and 1930. It's interesting to compare the times of the earliest Derby winners with present-day records: Mick the Miller's fastest Derby time over the 525 yards was 29.96 sec. A new record of 29.62 was set by Future Cutlet in 1932, The latest record has been held by Yellow Printer since 1968 with 28.30, while in 1958 Pigalle Wonder covered the same course in 28.44.

A racing Greyhound that caught the imagination of the public in 1971 was Dolores Rocket, a black bitch admired every bit as much for her beauty as for her track record. She won the Derby in 1971 and was the first female to win the classic since Narrogar Ann in 1949. The latter bitch was trained by the late Leslie Reynolds, who turned out five Derby winners, including Endless Gossip. Dolores Rocket was whelped in March 1969 and is owned, bred and trained by Mr Bert White, who was voted top trainer for 1971. Like Mick the Miller and Pigalle Wonder, she drew the public in enormous numbers every time she ran and collected a total of £15,066 in prize money. She has been painted for posterity by the well-known artist Leesa Sandys-Lumsdaine.

That a bitch so successful on the track can also be exceptionally beautiful gives one hope that the breed may unite again, but any realist must have grave doubts. For a dog to take part in all three activities — showing, racing and coursing — the owner would need to work a twenty-four-hour day. If the show breeders would outcross to the coursing or racing stock, the situation might become easier, but if quality were lost in the effort, the project would be defeated before it began. Plainly there is no hope that the racing and coursing breeders would want to use show stock, since looks are totally unimportant to them, so there is no alternative but to accept and admire the three types for the immense entertainment, sport and beauty that they contribute to the canine world.

Miss Pamela Vogel is the secretary of the Greyhound Club. Her address is: 9 Graveney Square, Cricketer's Way, Andover, Hants.

THE GREYHOUND STANDARD

Characteristics
The Greyhound possesses remarkable stamina and endurance, its straight-through, long-reaching movement enabling it to cover ground at great speed.

General appearance
The general appearance of the typical Greyhound is that of a strongly built, upstanding dog of generous proportions, muscular power and symmetrical formation, with a long head and neck, clean, well-laid shoulders, deep chest, capacious body, arched loins, powerful quarters, sound legs and feet, and a suppleness of limb, which emphasise to a marked degree its distinctive type and quality.

Head and skull
Long, moderate width, flat skull, slight stop. Jaws powerful and well chiselled.

Eyes
Bright and intelligent, dark in colour.

Ears
Small, rose-shaped, of fine texture.

Mouth
Teeth white and strong. The incisors of the upper jaw clipping those of the lower jaw.

Neck
Long and muscular, elegantly arched, well let into the shoulders.

Forequarters
Shoulders oblique, well set back, muscular without being loaded, narrow and cleanly defined at the top. Forelegs, long and straight, bone of good substance and quality. Elbows free and well set under the shoulders. Pasterns, moderate length,

slightly sprung. Elbows, pasterns and toes should incline neither outwards nor inwards.

Body
Chest, deep and capacious, providing adequate heart room. Ribs, deep, well sprung, and carried well back. Flanks well cut up. Back, rather long, broad and square. Loin, powerful, slightly arched.

Hindquarters
Thighs and second thighs, wide and muscular, showing great propelling power. Stifles, well bent. Hocks, well let down, inclining neither outwards nor inwards. Body and hindquarters should be of ample proportions and well coupled, enabling ground to be covered when standing.

Feet
Moderate length, with compact and well-knuckled toes, strong pads.

Tail
Long, set on rather low, strong at the root, tapering to the point, carried low, slightly curved.

Coat
Fine and close.

Colours
Black, white, red, blue, fawn, fallow, brindled, or any of the colours broken with white.

Height
Ideal: Dogs, 28 - 30 in.; Bitches 27 - 28 in.

10

The Irish Wolfhound

'Noble in character, majestic in bearing, swift in the chase, tenacious to the end, a mighty hunter, generous to friend but terrible to foe, supreme among the canine races for intelligence and an almost uncanny sense of good and evil, sublime in his devotion, the "joy of his master's heart" and faithful unto death.' That was Ralph Montagu's description of the Irish Wolfhound in the breed magazine bearing its name published in an issue of 1925.

As already stated, the background of the Irish Wolfhound is uncertain. We know that there were enormous wolf-dogs in Ireland as long ago as 391, but it is generally believed that they were very varied in colour, size and coat texture. The type that survived when wolves became extinct in 1770 was similar to the Deerhound, but smaller than the original wolf-dogs known the world over for their massive stature. By outcrossing with Great Danes, among other breeds, the size was restored so that the modern dog is the largest and heaviest of the Gazehound group.

Although it's easier to breed a Gazehound up in size than to achieve the reverse, it wasn't simple to produce the characteristic bulk of the Wolfhound out of a Deerhound. One of the major strains used was that of Glengarry, the breeder of Sir Walter Scott's bitch, Maida, who used various outcrosses to establish his particular brand of Deerhound. So one can safely say that when the dog was reconstructed about the middle of the nineteenth century, he consisted of a combination of various lines and breeds. When increasing the size, bone and substance are frequently lost, so it's possible that the Mastiff and Bloodhound crosses that have been suggested are authentic. The most interesting outcross put forward by past authorities is that of the wolf, but the characteristics of the Wolfhound and the Deerhound were so similar that one would have to include the latter in the same generalisation.

There is an account of an unsuccessful attempt to mate a wolf and a dog in captivity. This is mentioned in Father Hogan's book *The Irish Wolfdog*, in which he quotes from a magazine called *The Sportsman's Cabinet*. There seems to be no evidence of a successful mating between the two animals at any stage. Obviously this consideration would not have affected the breed's reconstruction in the nineteenth century, as the wolf had ceased to exist nearly a hundred years before. There is absolutely no reason, however, to prevent a dog and a wolf being mated. Farley Mowat, in his fascinating book *Never Cry Wolf,* which describes his experiences while researching wolves in the Antarctic, gives an account of an easily achieved union between a wolf and a Husky. In this case the latter was tethered outside the author's tent, where the wolf visited her. The tenacity and ardour of the wolf caused the situation to become more complicated, so that it was necessary for the Husky to be turned loose into the wild until the end of her season, when she returned quite happily to her owner. Unfortunately the author does not relate whether there were any puppies as a result of the mating.

Miss P. Gardner, in her book *The Irish Wolfhound,* says, on the subject of crosses, 'There were till the early part of the nineteenth century very widely divergent types of hounds, ranging from a heavy blood-hound-like Mastiff to a very slender Greyhound, and in all degrees of shagginess and smoothness, all used for hunting wolves in Ireland and therefore having the right to the name of Irish Wolf Dog . . . the only specimens of the Irish Wolf Dog that survived till the present day [the 1930s] were of a type resembling a rather heavy Deerhound.'

Through the centuries Irish Wolfhounds were favourite presents for monarchs and there are numbers of Irish legends on the subject in the breed books. Many of these are confusing as they might apply either to the Wolfhound or the Deerhound. Irish hounds were particularly sought after in Spain and at the time of Henry VIII it is reported that four were sent to that country each year. John of Poland was another king who imported a good number. Some say these hounds could pick out an Irish king among large numbers of people, others tell of them approaching total strangers because the dogs sensed that they were of royal blood! Like most Gazehounds, the Irish Greyhound was owned by royalty and the aristocracy and was much prized for his size and excellent properties as a guard. Not only would he hunt and kill wolves, but he would course the Irish Elk, reputed to be about six feet tall.

When numbers in the breed declined, as did those of the Deerhound, at the beginning of the last century, it was decided by the famous Captain Graham to try to revive the breed. He says:

About the year 1863, the writer took the Irish Wolfhound question up, and instituted very searching enquiries after any specimens of the breed. For some years he did not meet with much success; but about twelve years ago three distinct strains were brought to his notice, viz., those of the late Sir J. Power of Kilfane, the late Mr Baker of Ballytobin and Mr Mahoney of Dropmore — Alas! now all believed to be lost, save some of the descendants of the first two strains which are in the writer's hands and one or two other hands. Isolated specimens were also heard of, but none came under the writer's personal notice. It is believed that the Kilfane strain owed its origin partly to dogs bred by Richardson who, not content with writing, actually set to work to discover the breed; from him Sir John Power had more than one specimen. Richardson obtained bitches from Mr Carter of Bray (whose strain he mentioned in his essay) and crossing these with a grand dog of great height, produced some remarkably fine dogs. It is also believed that this strain was descended from Hamilton Rowan's dog, Bran, before mentioned.

Of this strain also were the Ballytobin dogs. Mr Baker was an enthusiast regarding all old Irish institutions, and having built himself a castle, he did all he could to increase the size of the deer in his park, also to restore to their original form, the Irish Wolfdogs. To this end he produced the best specimens, whenever to be had, regardless of cost, and at his death, some twelve years ago, he left a kennel of very fine dogs. The pick of these — bequeathed to a friend — a bitch, eventually came into the possession of the writer, and from her and from dogs of the writer's own breeding, his present strain has sprung . . .

Later, Graham says: . . .

It has been the steadfast endeavour of the writer to get crosses from such dogs of acknowledged Irish Wolfhound blood as were to be found, in preference to simply crossing opposite breeds to effect the desired object.

Several very fine dogs have been bred by the writer, but he has lost all the finest. He succeeded in rearing a remarkable dog that stood 33in. and was covered with a thick coat of nearly black shaggy hair. This dog unfortunately died at seventeen months of age, leaving behind him one litter of puppies, of which few remain.

I quote Graham at length because by doing so I hope the reader will understand and appreciate his care and great expense to save the Wolfhound from extinction. In his book of Irish Wolfhound pedigrees (compiled by Delphis Gardiner from his working stud book) there are photographs, drawings and descriptions of the majority of Irish Wolfhounds in existence in Graham's lifetime. These number about six hundred in all. There are comments on conformation and temperament after many of the names. For example, Mrs Gerard's Cheevra, whelped in June 1892, is listed and described as 'Blue brindle, poor coat — 28½in. Good bitch, rather Great Daney.' This lends weight to the theory that the Dane cross was used. Another, W. Spiller Allen's Orla, is said to be 'Red brindle. Good coat. Moderate. Too Deerhoundy.' Yet another, Rory Dhu, belonging to Miss Gibbons, is described as 'Dark brindle. Rough. 31½in. Good head and ears. Very handsome? Killed sheep.' Details of this sort are given with each dog.

From that book one can see that colour varied immensely.

One or two of the illustrations bear little resemblance to a Wolfhound, but these are in the minority. One male, owned by Major Shewell, Ch. Cotswold, was born in 1902 and must have come very close to Graham's ideal. In fact he was said to have remarked that he could find no fault in him. This dog stood 33in. to the shoulder and had a rough coat and, judging by his photograph, great presence. At the front of the book is a photograph of Graham with a Wolfhound model he had made. The height of this is 35in. and the weight should be 140lb, according to Graham's comments on the back of the original.

A second breeder should be remembered for keeping the breed alive, during World War I. This was Mr D. W. Everett of the famous Felixstowe prefix. During the last war Mrs E. James was one of the very few who managed to breed.

The first show classes for Irish Wolfhounds appear in the 1880 edition of the *Kennel Club Calendar and Stud Book*. They were scheduled at the Second Exhibition of Sporting and Other Dogs held by the Irish Kennel Club in Dublin in April 1879. Mr Hugh Dalziel was judging. First was Mr P. H. Cooper's Brian, second a dog for which no registration details are given, owned by Mr F. Adcock, and third Captain G. A. Graham's Scot. Brian's owner lived at Bulwell Hall, Nottingham, the breeder and age of the dog were unknown — he was by Swarram out of Linda. This particular Brian (there were many of that name and several also named Bran) is the forebear of the majority of today's dogs and measured 33in. Graham's dogs were always said to be light. Type varied tremendously at that time. Scot was owner-bred and whelped on 28 May 1877. He was by Oscar out of Juno. This dog had both the Kilfane and Ballytobin strains from Ireland behind him.

At the Kennel Club's Seventh Exhibition at Crystal Palace in June, 1881, the judge was Mr Vere Shaw. The winner was W. de Jessop's Hydra, who was by the Brian mentioned above, and second Captain Graham's Clutha.

O'Leary was another dominant sire of that period; he, Brian I and Graham's Brian II (bred quite differently from Brian I) were said to have Great Dane blood.

Of the more recent dogs and their influence on the breed
of today, Mrs Nagle's Ch. Sulhamstead Concara must be one
of the most famous. He was born blind and was going to be
destroyed, but Mrs Nagle took him from the nest at six weeks
and campaigned him in the show ring. He gained his title
and it was not generally known that he was blind until he was
retired from showing. He was a very influential sire, one of
the most beautiful of his sons being Galleon of Ouborough.
Of the modern dogs, the same owner's Ch. Sulhamstead
Match will go down as one of the greatest sires. He is behind
ten out of twelve of the champions photographed in the Irish
Wolfhound Club's year book for the years 1967-9. These
include Sulhamstead Morna of Eaglescrag, Baldeagle Fiona
of Eaglescrag and Boroughbury Brona. Both challenge
certificates at Cruft's in 1973 were won by the Sulhamstead
kennel. Ch. Sulhamstead Major was best of breed and Ch.
Sulhamstead Modena took the bitch certificate. Another
great dog in the breed is Ch. Eaglescrag Caio, owned and
bred by Mr and Mrs Jenkins, winner of the club trophy for
the most points gained at championship shows for two
successive years recently.

Part of the success of the modern hounds stems from two
dogs imported from the United States when there was need
for new blood. Both made a very necessary impact. In 1952
Miss F. J. McGregor presented Rory of Kihone to the club.
He was placed in the kennel of the Misses Harrison and
Atfield of the well-known Sanctuary prefix and became an
English champion. He was used at stud a good deal and
appears in most modern pedigrees. In 1955 the second hound
was presented by Mrs Peter van Brunt to the same kennel.
This was American Ch. Cragwood Barney O'Shea of Riverlawn. He sired several litters, but unfortunately died shortly
after his quarantine period was over.

Today the Wolfhound doesn't have the chance to work very
much either in Europe or America, though Miss Hudson of
East Dereham in Norfolk, owner of the top Wolfhound for
1973, Ch. Petasmeade Chieftain of Brabyns, tells me she has
coursed her dogs at a Saluki/Deerhound meeting in Scotland
and uses them for rabbiting at home. She finds they are

much faster than generally supposed and can pick up a hare or rabbit very easily. Her family have hunted fox successfully with Wolfhounds and Salukis in Ireland.

In *The Irish Wolfhound* of September 1925 there is an account of Wolfhound field trials and coursing held at Pippingford Park, Nutley, Sussex. The winners of the two trials were Mrs Massy's Maureen of Ifold and Mr Wade's Kathleen-na-Houlihan. The hare coursing took place after lunch and the ten-dog stake was won by Captain Hudson's Colleen of Brabyns.

The same magazine contains an article by Mary Beynon in which she gives a description of how, when living in Kenya, her three Irish Wolfhounds defended her and chased off a lioness and two cubs that she had come upon eating a stag. Without hesitation all three dogs rushed to her defence so that she was able to walk on unharmed. An interesting theory put forward in this same article is that the hound with the light eye is the bravest in battle. Mary Beynon says 'Present day shows are making a big mistake in penalising light eyes and so helping to breed out courage. If your life depends upon the quick responding to your call for help—even to attacking a lion—if the lion won't run — I would always pick a light-eyed hound if it was to be my life which was to be so tested.' Many Gazehound owners claim that light-eyed hounds are the most persistent hunters and difficult to keep at home; but a number of judges dislike anything but a dark eye, even though it is not stipulated in all breed Standards. Very light eyes are, however, listed in the Wolfhound Standard under faults.

In 1934 the Irish Wolfhound Club was formed and meetings were held from that year until 1938. The winners and their breeding may be of interest to readers and are as follows:

FIRST MEETING HELD AT SULHAMSTEAD 23 JANUARY 1934

Springhill Stakes Open Dogs
Winner: Lady Watson's Sulhamstead Cato. Sire: Ch. Felix-stowe Killary. Dam: Sulhamstead Cherie.

Broadway Stakes Open Bitches
Winner: Mrs Cuttle's Hawthorne Aileen. Sire: Connemara
Ouborough. Dam: Aileen of Bramblestown.

The Coolafin Open Dog Stakes
Winner: Lady Watson's Sulhamstead Cato. Sire: Ch. Felix-
stowe Killary. Dam: Sulhamstead Cherie.

The Sulhamstead Stakes Open Bitches
Winner: Mrs Nagle's Sulhamstead Kyra. Sire: Sulhamstead
Caesar. Dam: Sulhamstead Kiwi.

The Novice Stakes for Dogs and Bitches
Winner: Mrs Nagle's Sulhamstead Krim. Sire: Sulhamstead
Caesar. Dam: Sulhamstead Kiwi.

Open Stakes for Dogs and Bitches
Winner: Mrs Nagle's Sulhamstead Finn. Sire: Ch. Fion-mac-
cumall of Brabyns. Dam: Ch. Sulhamstead Diana.

The Coolafin Stakes Open Dogs
Winner: Mrs Cuttle's Ch. Faithful Grey. Sire: Connemara of
Ouborough. Dam: Aileen of Ben Edar.

The Sulhamstead Stakes Open Bitches
Winner: Mrs Cuttle's Hawthorne Keady. Sire: Finn of
Ardeen. Dam: Hawthorn Aileen.

The Novice Stakes Dogs and Bitches
Winner: Mrs Nagle's Sulhamstead Rita. Sire: Sulhamstead
Krim. Dam: Rippingdon Rathgalleon.

Open Dog Stakes
Winner: Mrs Nagle's Sulhamstead Finn. Sire: Ch. Fion-mac-cumall of Brabyns. Dam: Ch. Sulhamstead Diana.

Open Bitch Stakes
Winner: Miss Ansell's Sgeolan of Ouborough. Sire: Ch. Farnoge of Ouborough. Dam: Conna of Ouborough.

SIXTH MEETING 16 JANUARY 1937

The Pentavalon Stakes, Novice Dogs and Bitches
Winner: Mrs Alan Stoddart's Woodsmoke. Sire: Ch. Faithful Grey. Dam: Findebar of Brabyns.

The Sulhamstead Open Stakes Dogs and Bitches
Winner: Mrs Nagle's Sulhamstead Finn. Sire: Ch. Fion-mac-cumall of Brabyns. Dam: Ch. Sulhamstead Diana.

The Novice Stakes Dogs and Bitches
Winner: Miss S. Stoddart's Banba of Brabyns. Sire: Ch. Rippingdon Dan of Southwick. Dam: Steyning Lisa.

The Brabyns Stakes Open Dogs
Winner: Mrs Nagle's Sulhamstead Finn. Sire: Ch. Fion-mac-cumall of Brabyns. Dam: Ch. Sulhamstead Diana.

Gammaton Stakes Open Bitches
Winner: Mrs Alan Stoddart's Woodsmoke. Sire: Ch. Faithful Grey. Dam: Findebear of Brabyns.

EIGHTH MEETING 22 JANUARY 1938

The Pentavlon Novice Stakes
Winner: Miss Addie's Aifa of Brabyns. Sire: Knuckles. Dam: Taran of Brabyns.

Open Dog Stakes
Winner: Mrs Nagle's Sulhamstead Finn. Sire: Ch. Fion-mac-
cumall of Brabyns. Dam: Ch. Sulhamstead Diana.

The Sulhamstead Stakes Open Bitches
Winners: Divided
Mrs Alan Stoddart's Woodsmoke. Sire: Ch. Faithful Grey.
Dam: Findebar of Brabyns.
Miss Stoddart's Banba of Brabyns. Sire: Ch. Rippingdon Dan
of Southwick. Dam: Steyning Lisa.

These results are taken from the Irish Wolfhound Club
Year Books for 1935-7.

In Mrs Alma Starbuck's recent American-published book,
The Complete Irish Wolfhound, there are further accounts of
Wolfhounds coursing bears, prairie wolves, jack rabbits,
kangaroos, wallabies and deer. In the January-March 1973
issue of the breed magazine, Joan Milnes tells how she trained
her first Irish Wolfhound to retrieve and track so that it could
eventually compete successfully in Open Working Trials with
her Alsatians. The Wolfhound is amazingly versatile. Unfortunately this trailing and coursing event of the 1920s was
not repeated, despite its success, so few of these dogs have
been coursed competitively since then.

Not only are Wolfhounds brave and even fierce in
dangerous situations, but they are also extremely gentle and
utterly trustworthy with children. At shows one frequently
sees them being hugged, or sat on by children who are
strange to them, but these enormous dogs react in a consistently kind manner.

There is one further use for them which should not be
forgotten. The Irish Guards have owned an Irish Wolfhound,
first as a regimental pet, then as a mascot, since the
beginning of the century. The latest to be presented to the
regiment by the Irish Wolfhound Club in 1967 was Samada
Silver, and in 1966 the Club invited the Regimental Lieute-
nant-Colonel to be its President.

As has happened for all the hound breeds, Irish Wolfhound registration figures at the Kennel Club are rising and

there is evidence of indiscriminate breeding by the inexperienced. Mrs Jenkins of the Eaglescrag prefix runs a rescue service and places about four hounds per annum in new homes. Each dog is vetted before it is placed and papers are never provided with it. Puppy farms are beginning to deal in Wolfhounds and there is great concern among the conscientious members of the breed that these beautiful dogs will lose their excellent type and characteristics if the trend continues. There is always the danger that the public will, unknowingly, buy from the less reputable — thus ruining a sound breed. It has taken time, trouble and expense to build the excellent modern specimen and it would be appalling if he was ruined by the commercial market.

There is only one club for the Wolfhound and the secretary is: Mrs Helen Baird, Berry Corner, Berry Lane, Chorleywood, Herts.

THE IRISH WOLFHOUND STANDARD

General appearance
The Irish Wolfhound should not be quite so heavy or as massive as the Great Dane, but more so than the Deerhound, which in general type he should otherwise resemble. Of great size and commanding appearance, very muscular, strongly although gracefully built, movements easy and active; head and neck carried high; the tail carried with an upward sweep with a slight curve towards the extremity.

Height and weight
The minimum height and weight of dogs should be 31in. and 120lb; of bitches 28in. and 90lb. Anything below this should be debarred from competition. Great size, including height at shoulder and proportionate length of body, is to be aimed for, and it is desired to establish, firmly, a race that shall average from 32 to 34in. in dogs, showing the requisite power, activity, courage and symmetry.

Head and skull
Long, the frontal bones of the forehead very slightly raised and very little indentation between the eyes. Skull, not too broad. Muzzle, long and moderately pointed. Ears, small and Greyhound-like in carriage.

Neck
Rather long, very strong and muscular, well arched, without dewlap or loose skin about the throat.

Chest
Very deep. Breast wide.

Back
Rather long than short. Loins arched.

Tail
Long and slightly curved, of moderate thickness, and well covered with hair.

Belly
Well drawn up.

Forequarters
Shoulders muscular, giving breadth of chest, set sloping. Elbows well under, neither turned inwards nor outwards. Leg. Forearm muscular and the whole leg strong and straight.

Hindquarters
Muscular thighs and second thigh long and strong as in the Greyhound; hocks well let down and turning neither in nor out.

Feet
Moderately large and round, turned neither inwards nor outwards. Toes, well arched and closed. Nails very strong and curved.

Hair
Rough and hard on body, legs and head; especially wiry and long over eyes and under jaw.

Above, Mr. Donald Wieden's International Saluki Champion Sedeki Barre; *below*, Mrs. Wilton-Clark's Whippet bitch, Champion Sequence of Shalfleet, who has won twelve challenge certificates

Above, Mr. Gordon Wigg's black/white Whippet dog, Champion Ladiesfield Bedazzled. Many show and racing winners are line bred to him; *below*, three of the author's Whippets. All have the far-seeing eye, vital to the Gazehound

Kamee von Ali Baba, who set and held a new European racing record for Afghans in the late 1960s; *below*, Continental Greyhounds leave the traps at the start of a race

Above, Mr. John Bisek's Chapi, a highly successful racing Greyhound in Czechoslovakia; *below*, a Whippet racing at the Renbaan Ookmeer track in Amsterdam

Colour and markings
The recognised colours are: grey, brindle, red, black, pure white, fawn, or any colour that appears in the Deerhound.

Faults
Too light or heavy head; too highly arched frontal bone; large ears and hanging flat to the face; short neck; excess dewlap; too narrow or too broad a chest; sunken, hollow or quite straight back; bent forelegs; overbent fetlocks; twisted feet; spreading toes; too curly a tail; weak hindquarters and a general lack of muscle; too short in body; pink or liver-coloured eyelids; lips and nose any colour other than black; very light eyes.

11

The Lurcher

No book on long dogs would be complete without a chapter on the Lurcher, the true Romany hound. His name is derived from the Romany word meaning to rob or plunder. Even though he is a cross-bred he is certainly not a mongrel and is normally threequarters sighthound. The Lurcher is, of course, an intentional breed cross with a Greyhound or a Whippet. The most popular combination used to be the Sheepdog/Greyhound cross, but today the gipsies seem to prefer the Deerhound/Greyhound cross which produces a combination of speed, height, brains and a harsh coat. The Sheepdog crosses frequently failed to produce the necessary size, although the progeny invariably had the coarse coat. The Lurcher is traditionally a working dog, so a wiry coat is essential. The fine, silken skin of the Greyhound tears too easily on wire and thick cover.

At one time a variety called the Norfolk Lurcher was much prized. This was a combination of the Smithfield Cattle Dog and Greyhound. The Smithfields were rough-coated Sheepdogs used to drive stock to Smithfield Market from East Anglia. Their descendants are frequently light and even white in colour. Although there were Lurchers of this variety twenty or thirty years ago, the cross can no longer be used because the Smithfield as such has ceased to exist, but the strain is still behind many modern Lurchers. Unfortunately there is a tendency to call any rough-coated Lurcher a 'Norfolk' and many breeders are quite ignorant of the meaning of the term.

The Deerhound cross is always referred to by travelling men as a 'stag' cross. The addition of Greyhound blood to this breed produces the extra speed. Salukis are also used by the gipsies because they provide extra stamina, but the coat of the resulting progeny is not sufficiently rough.

114

The Greyhound Lurcher is the only one that the gipsies will consider seriously because they claim that the Whippet, although excellent for rabbiting, hasn't the stamina for a day's hare coursing. The Greyhound, because of his size, can frequently reach his neck out for the kill without needing to make the further effort of turning as does a smaller dog.

Lurchers must be clever enough to hunt silently and, contrary to most training methods, the poacher teaches his hound to go home when whistled and to drop his quarry away from, but in sight of, his master if the latter is talking to a stranger. The hare or rabbit will be collected later when the coast is clear. The dog should also be able to retrieve game, which is why a Retriever cross is occasionally used, with preference for the leggier breeds, such as Flatcoats, because the Labrador or Golden Retriever crosses tend to be too heavy or too slow.

Gypsy training methods are frowned on in some Lurcher circles because puppies start to work at the early age of six months. Instead of the older and more correct practice of waiting until the dog is fully grown, a puppy is released when the quarry is captured by the older hounds and when it is still kicking. This encourages the killing instinct, without which no working hound is of any value. If, after half-a-dozen outings, the dog when adult has not killed the expected number of hares or rabbits, he is sold on, sometimes at a grossly inflated price, depending on the guile of the owner. Lurchers used to change hands in large numbers at the famous Brough and Appleby Horse Fairs in the North of England. Twenty years ago puppies were sometimes sold for as little as £2, but now, although it is still possible to buy an untried puppy, the price can be astronomical.

In the words of Andrew Simpson, in his book Rebecca the Lurcher, in which he admits to being a novice on the subject, he says, quite rightly: He [the Lurcher] should have the speed of a Greyhound, the nose of a Foxhound, and the eye of a hawk. Although built for speed, he should not flinch at thorns and thickets and barbed wire, nor at heavy plough underfoot, nor at the cold of long winter days and nights in the open. Although bred to hunt, he should be intelligent enough to learn not to worry sheep or chase cattle, and to be utterly still when he is told to be utterly still. He may growl, but he should seldom bark. For him the eleventh commandment is 'Thou shalt not be caught.' In fact, a Lurcher is a hungry poacher's dog which is no easy role to play.''

Unfortunately, when experiments are made with any canine cross, some of the progeny revert to one or other of the parents. Only a few have the best qualities of both. It is thus that one sees so many smooth-coated Lurchers when the real purpose of the breed, as already mentioned, is to produce a harsher, denser coat than has the Greyhound or Whippet. Picking a small puppy unerringly is almost impossible, as the harsh coat frequently develops late. A long body is vital, combined with intelligence, guts and character. These qualities stand out even in a very young puppy and, if in doubt, they are the ones to aim for.

All gipsies love a long dog and one never ceases to be amazed by their knowledge and the eye they have for a good coursing hound. 'Lurcher' is not a term used by these people. They refer to their hounds by the name of the cross used to produce them — 'Stag', 'Saluki' etc. They pay enormous sums for really good, proved adult hounds, although these are very hard to come by.

Lurcher owners are often responsible for losing a good ground used by the followers of organised coursing. The fact that the land is poached by any owner of long dogs tends to turn the landowner against even the most respectable coursing enthusiasts. It's undeniable that Lurcher people seem unable to stop poaching — probably because it provides extra excitement.

Because his make-up is composed very largely of sighthound, the Lurcher, like his ancestors, scans the landscape before he makes a move, but, depending on the cross used to produce him, his excellent eyesight is frequently combined with keen scenting powers. He will cover a field, using both methods of discovering the quarry, and will work the hedgerows as well as the open plough or stubble.

There is a new and immense upsurge in support for the Lurcher now that a show devoted to the breed has been held

at Lambourn in August for the last three years. The aims of
the organisers have been to combine several events to
encourage all the best of their remarkable qualities. The
promotors were Mrs Peter Lowis and the artist Miss Leesa
Sandys-Lumsdaine. Sometimes the proceeds go to the Injured
Jockey Fund and on other occasions to the World Wild Life
Fund. There are show classes for rough- and smooth-coated
hounds, as well as for puppies and veterans. About a couple
of hundred dogs are usually entered. After the show classes
there are obstacle and high-jump courses to be negotiated,
obedience tests and racing. The latter is the real test of the
renowned Lurcher temperament. The dogs are normally
slipped by their owners and run without muzzles. Despite the
fact that all shapes and sizes of long dogs run together, there
is virtually no fighting of any sort. In contrast, other breeds,
such as Terriers and Gundogs, run at the end of the day, and
the fighting is then so appalling that no race is completed!
The gipsies watch all the show classes with great interest and
frequently approach owners with a view to buying their
exhibits.

At the first Lurcher show the two judges had varying opinions
on the qualities they sought in a Lurcher. The first held out
for a good jaw, a broad head set on a long neck, good length
and arch of loin and well-let-down hocks. The second stressed
the importance of a long strong back, good spring of rib, a
hard eye and well-knuckled-up feet. Eyes in Lurchers are a
particularly interesting feature because they are renowned for
being yellow. This colour, however, is penalised in certain
Gazehound breeds, for which a dark eye is stipulated. In the
breeds, however, for which a light eye is accepted, owners
frequently claim that the yellow eye sees further and denotes
a courageous temperament.

A favourite name for Lurchers is 'dinner snatchers' and
plainly they are well named. I quote from *Of Pedigree
Unknown*, by Phil Drabble, who has owned several types of
Lurcher. In this particular extract he describes the habits of
his Lurcher Gypsy, a Greyhound/Deerhound cross:

Her table manners left something to be desired too. We
were sitting round the fire eating afternoon tea from little

tables and making polite conversation with a somewhat
starchy guest. Gypsy lay by the fire and moved because she
got too hot. She timed her journey so that she passed the
guest's table as he turned his head to speak. Without
faltering in her stride, she nicked the sandwich from his
plate as smoothly as a conjuror. He never even noticed, so I
offered him another. Three minutes later she had that
and, his hands groping for it as he talked, a slightly puzzled
expression did flit across his face. He appeared worried
that he was getting absent minded so I passed him the
plate and he took another without a word. Even then, with
his suspicions half aroused, she took the third without
actually getting caught; but it made me laugh and it gave
the game away.

Some years ago there was a possibility that now, in this the
age of the motor caravan, the Lurcher would decrease in
numbers. Yet there seem to be more about now than ever
before. Traditionally they hunt for their owner's pot but
above all they provide the travelling man with sport. No
Sunday morning would be the same without the betting on
which dog is the fastest, the best stayer or the master of the
most hares.

12

The Pharaoh Hound

It is extraordinary that the Pharaoh Hound has remained undiscovered by British breeders until quite recently. Although one or two of these hounds were imported in 1936 the breed did not become established until Mrs Block, Mrs Liddell Grainger and Mrs Michael Dewey brought more into this country in 1963. In 1968, Mr Hamilton Renwick imported a dog and three bitches. One of the latter was aged eight and he first saw her sleeping on a doorstep on the Island of Gozo. Mrs Block believes that Pharaoh Hounds were not imported previously because Malta was a British naval and military base. Coming from a nation of dog-lovers, it would have been impracticable for service personal to bring hounds home because of the quarantine laws and the postings to different parts of the world that servicemen often have during the course of their careers. It was only when Malta and Gozo became tourist centres that the attention of the general public was drawn to these unusual dogs. On both islands they are to be seen sunbathing in the streets.

Originally the Pharaoh Hound came from Egypt with Phoenecian traders, and, because, until fairly recently, neither Malta nor Gozo had an influx of either people or dogs from other nations the Pharaohs have been bred pure for generations. The typical red colouring with flesh-coloured nose and white chest have persisted down the centuries. These hounds are exported with papers because the Malta Kennel Club is affiliated to the British Kennel Club. Many Maltese know from memory the breeding of their hounds. The national name for them on the island is *Kelp Tal Fenech* which, translated, means 'Rabbit Dog' and the native sportsmen use them for just that purpose.

The dogs work either at night or very early in the morning.

Most fields in Malta are surrounded by walls, under which the rabbits tend to collect. Much of the surface of the ground is very hard going and either rocky or stony. The hounds, loosed in small numbers, find the rabbits, which are then driven out by ferrets into a net. The rabbits that escape are killed by the waiting dogs. Bitches are more popular for work then dogs.

Another method used for just a pair of dogs is a *Kurriera*. Both hounds go in opposite directions and methodically work their way round in a circle, flushing rabbits from boundary walls, vines and scrub as they go. Finally they meet up again with their owner at the original starting point. When they hunt in pairs like this the local term for it is *Mizzewgn*, which means 'united in pairs'.

As can so many Gazehounds, the Pharaoh scales a 7ft wall with ease. He is more muscular than the show Greyhound and has excellent stamina. Considering the surface he works over, he is extremely fast and is sometimes used for wild deer as he is tall enough to tackle an animal of this size. His agility is as exceptional as his hearing. It is an interesting fact that Pharaohs are the only members of the Gazehound group with erect ears. One has only to watch them hunt to discover the reason for this. They listen for the quarry after looking first. Upright ears are penalised in the show ring in every other sighthound. In the Pharaoh a folded ear is a great fault. Some of the other breeds in the group even stipulate a dropped ear. That Ibizan Hound owners claim their dogs are not sighthounds, as they hunt primarily by sound, presumably results from the fact that the hearing in these animals, close relatives of the Pharaoh, is even more highly developed and their breeders work to this end.

A show for Pharaoh Hounds is held once a year in Malta, but, as they are kept primarily for working purposes, few dogs are exhibited. There is now the very real danger that, with the development of the tourist trade in Malta and Gozo, they will be out-crossed with other breeds visiting the islands. The Maltese, however, would not tolerate this and would put down any result of a misalliance, so while the breed remains in their hands it is safe.

Not only are the dogs good rabbiters, but they are also excellent guard dogs. They are frequently to be seen prowling round the low parapets of the farmhouse flat roofs, protecting the household in an owner's absence. Their deep, baying bark would frighten off any intruder. Many of the Maltese keep their hounds in rough conditions, but there is very little variation in coat texture. Lionel Hamilton-Renwick, in an article in *The Field* (27 February 1969), says that the eight-year old bitch referred to earlier was covered with ticks and fleas, which would indicate she had been living out.

Mrs Block saw her first Pharaoh Hound tied up outside a garage in Malta while she was on holiday there, and thought him beautiful. The Maltese are wary over parting with their hounds, because each proud owner wants his Pharaoh to be the best. Competition is, therefore, keen, which is beneficial to the breed and a joy to the owner of the best hound. Furthermore, for sporting purposes an owner depends greatly on his dog. After considerable bartering, Mrs Block managed to buy her Pharaoh because the owner was leaving for England. He was called *Bahri,* which is Maltese for 'sailor.' Unfortunately he sired only one litter before disappearing while out rabbiting. His owner discovered years later, and after many enquiries, that he had been shot by a local gamekeeper. Mrs Block and other enthusiasts have since imported more Pharaohs and the breed is increasing in numbers: there are about 350 Pharaohs in Britain at present.

The emblem of the Pharaoh Hound Club is taken from the tomb of Antefa II, from the XIth Dynasty—dating from 2,300 *BC* approximately. It shows a dog of rangey build, not quite as big as a Greyhound, with erect ears and a ringed tail held high over its back. It is wearing a very elaborate, white-metal collar. Greyhound types with high ear-carriage have been depicted on the walls of Egyptian tombs since 4,000 *BC*, and the Pharaoh can, with justification, claim to be every bit as ancient as the Greyhound and the Saluki.

As stated elsewhere, research shows that, with three exceptions, most Gazehounds have been in existence from the same very early period. Only size, coat and ears varied, just as they do today.

Although the Pharaoh is a new breed in Britain, it has been established for some time on the Continent and is recognised by the Fédération Cynologique Internationale, which governs the show scene in most European countries. Scandinavia has recently imported some good specimens, as has America, where a breed club has just been formed with Mrs Rita Laventhall-Sacks as secretary. She herself bred the first international champion, Beltara's Amun-Re, which was exported to Mexico. Some 250 Pharaohs are registered in the USA and Canada has fifty. It seems, therefore, that their qualities are at last being appreciated, so it is to be hoped that all enthusiasts will continue to develop their excellent working ability.

A Standard of Points was first published in Hutchinson's Encyclopaedia in the 1930s. The British Standard was passed and published by the Kennel Club in December 1974. Challenge certificates were awarded for the first time at Cruft's 1975 and the first two champions were Miss Still's Kilcroney Rekhmire Merymut, who is by Twinley King Ka'a out of Kilcroney Senjura, and Mrs Waugh's Tarnach Twinley Xamxi who is also by King Ka'a out of Twinley Haddieda. It is interesting that both hounds have a large amount of Mrs Block's original Twinley breeding.

The secretary of the Breed Club is: Miss Monica Still, of the Merymut prefix, and her address is: 4 Lansdowne Road, Bedford.

THE PHARAOH HOUND STANDARD

Characteristics
An intelligent, friendly, affectionate, playful and alert breed. An alert and keen hunter, the Pharaoh Hound hunts by scent and sight, using its large ears to a marked degree when working close.

General appearance
The Pharaoh Hound is medium-sized, of noble bearing with clean-cut lines. Graceful yet powerful. Very fast with free, easy movement.

Head and skull
Skull long, lean and well-chiselled. Foreface slightly longer than the skull. Only slight stop. Top of skull parallel with the foreface, the whole head representing a blunt wedge when viewed in profile and from above.

Eyes
Amber-coloured, blending with the coat; oval, moderately deep set, with keen, intelligent expression.

Ears
Medium-high set; carried erect when alert, but very mobile; broad at the base, fine and large.

Mouth
Powerful jaws with strong teeth. Scissor bite.

Nose
Flesh-coloured only, blending with the coat.

Neck
Long, lean, muscular and slightly arched. Clean throat line.

Forequarters
Shoulders — strong, lean and well laid back. Forelegs — straight and parallel. Elbows well tucked in. Pasterns strong.

Body
Lithe with almost straight topline, slight slope down from croup to root of tail. Deep brisket extending down to point of elbow. Ribs well sprung. Moderate cut up. Length of body from breast to haunch bone slightly longer than height at withers.

Hindquarters
Strong and muscular. Moderate bend of stifle. Well-developed second thigh. Limbs parallel when viewed from behind.

Feet
Strong, well knuckled and firm, turning neither in nor out.
Paws well padded. Dew claws may be removed.

Gait
Free and flowing; the head should be held fairly high and the
dog should cover the ground well without any apparent
effort. The legs and feet should move in line with the body;
any tendency to throw the feet sideways, or a high-stepping
'hackney' action is a definite fault.

Tail
Medium set — fairly thick at the base and tapering (whip-
like), reaching just below the hock in repose. Carried high
and curved when the dog is in action. The tail should not be
tucked between the legs. A screw tail is a fault.

Coat
Short and glossy, ranging from fine and close to slightly
harsh; no feathering.

Colour
Tan or rich tan with white markings allowed as follows: white
tip on tail strongly desired; white on chest (called 'The Star');
white on toes; slim white blaze on centre line of face
permissible; flecking or white other than above undesirable.

Height
Dogs: ideally 56cm. (22-25in.); *Bitches:* ideally 53cm.
(21-24in.). Overall balance must be maintained.

Faults
Any deviation from the foregoing is a fault, hunting blemishes
excepted.

Note
Male animals should have two apparently normal testicles,
fully descended into the scrotum.

13

The Saluki

Unlike some of the Gazehound breeds, there is evidence that the Saluki was a contemporary of the Greyhound, and it is particularly interesting that a pair of Salukis appear on one of the enamelled funeral boxes found in the tomb of Tutankhamen. This is illustrated in an informative book *The Saluki in History, Art and Sport* by Hope and David Waters. The photograph shows Tutankhamen conquering Syrian enemies. There is also a carving of four Salukis in the tomb of the eleventh-dynasty Pharaoh Wahenkh Intef (2,222-2,271 *BC*) at Karnak. The dogs are called White Gazelle, Greyhound, Black and Firepot.

Varying types of Saluki can be found in Saudi Arabia, Persia, Syria and North Africa. The further south one travels the more one encounters lighter feathering. The North African variety is almost smooth.

The word *Slughi* is the Arabic for Greyhound, so the name probably originated in this part of the world. *Sagi-i-Tazi* is the term used for the breed in Persia and means Arabian Hound. In old prints one finds Salukis referred to as Persian Greyhounds. A typical example is James Ward's painting of Lady St George's Saluki, reproduced in *The Sporting Magazine* of 1907 with the caption 'Persian Greyhound'. Landseer's famous painting of Prince Albert's dog is frequently described as depicting a Greyhound, but the animal is quite definitely a black and cream Saluki. Presumably Landseer himself could tell the difference between the two breeds, because he had painted Salukis in their native surroundings.

The dogs from the Arabian Gulf are small and not well nourished because of the sparse vegetation and the often intense heat. They also have scanty coats. Action photographs taken in the desert show feathering on the tail and ears only. The Persian animals from the north are heavier, bigger and more feathered, to enable them to exist in the cooler climate. The Syrian dogs are very similar to this variety, presumably as a result of a similar environment. The Afghan, a Saluki cousin, and found even further north, has developed a correspondingly heavier coat.

The Arabian dogs, belonging to the wandering tribes of Bedouins, can exist for two or three weeks consecutively on a diet of milk. Their owners eat little more and the Salukis are prized above all other possessions because they provide food for the Bedouin families.

The dogs hunt on their own or are taken in pairs after desert hares and partridges. Gazelle are not available in such large numbers as they were twenty or thirty years ago, for a number of reasons. The vegetation has deteriorated as a result of goat overgrazing. Hunting methods, because of mechanisation, have altered. The rifle is now commonplace and consequently the quarry has been decimated. So sacred is the Saluki to the Bedouin that the puppies are even suckled by the women during particularly hard times. They are the only animals allowed inside the tents with their owners.

The Saluki has more stamina than any other member of the Gazehound family. For this reason, among others, he is the favourite of the Middle-Eastern sheiks who frequently entertain their guests by taking them on a chase after roebuck or the scarce gazelle. The Saluki is capable of coursing his quarry for hours on end and in scorching temperatures over red-hot sand and uneven, rocky terrain. The gazelle is worn down by the dogs' sheer endurance, although, on occasion, a hawk is used to bait and confuse the quarry by pecking at and hovering over its head.

It is said that a gazelle is capable of a speed of 45mph, but it tires before the Saluki. Sometimes, during a very long course, several pairs of dogs are taken out and fresh pairs are slipped to wear the hunted animal down more quickly. The gazelle is usually flushed by a servant on foot and, once in the open, is followed by the Sheik and his guests on horseback. The riders wait, tense and expectant, for the start of the chase. The dogs are also slipped by men on foot.

As happened with the Afghan, two different types of Saluki were brought to England and it is from a combination of both sorts that today's Saluki has emerged. The first type — the lighter, desert variety — was introduced a considerable time before the second, by the Hon. Florence Amherst at the end of the last century. When the Saluki Club was founded in 1923 this breeder became its first president. Miss Amherst was a great authority on the breed and wrote a number of articles on the subject for canine magazines and books.

The second type was imported by Brigadier and Mrs Lance after World War I. Their dog, Ch. Sarona Kelb, became one of the most influential sires in this country. He was a Syrian dog, and therefore had the characteristic sturdy build with a thick coat. His stock tended to be darker in colour because he was predominantly black with pale points, whereas Miss Amherst's dogs were a rich-red or a pale-golden colour. Kelb had a great effect on the show scene and sired many champions in the breed.

The first of these was a bitch, Ch. Orchard Shahin; she was also the first Saluki to gain a title in this country. She was owned by Mrs L. Crouch and bred by Brigadier Lance. Shahin won ten certificates and was the result of a brother and sister mating. Both her sire, Kelb, and her dam, Sarona Sarona, were by Seleughi out of Baalbek, who were Middle-Eastern animals. Shahin's first certificate was awarded in 1923. Kelb also sired Sarona Gulshere, a dog, and Sarona Gemil, a bitch, both of whom won ten challenge certificates, a remarkable achievement at that time.

The majority of the modern show and coursing dogs carry Kelb's bloodlines. He excelled in the field, as well as in the ring, and had killed several gazelle in Israel before he was brought here. He was also the second champion to be made up in Britain and won twelve challenge certificates, the last of which was awarded when he was eleven, a year before his death.

In the last ten years there have not been many imports from the East, although British breeders are generally keen to keep Eastern bloodlines in their stock. In 1957, Mr and Mrs Henderson of the Kumasi prefix brought two Salukis to this country, one of them smooth. Both were brought from Persia. The smooth bitch was called Kumasi Dhiba and her name appears in the pedigree of nearly all smooth-coated Salukis in this country. She came to the Hendersons when they were in Amarah, as a tiny puppy, looking Mrs Henderson told me — exactly like a tiny Arab horse. She was escorted by eight fully armed Arabs from Sheik Chassib Miftim from Nazimyah on the Persia-Iraq border to Amarah.

The dog, Kumasi Rihan, was feathered and came from Sheik Shakker Kommondan of Iraq. He was one of the Sheik's favourite Salukis as he was an excellent worker and had killed more than forty gazelle by the time he was eighteen months old. Rihan was brought to Mr and Mrs Henderson personally by the Sheik, and was accompanied by a kennelman who could recite the dog's pedigree back over several generations. The new owners were also presented with the pedigrees of both hounds, written out and signed in Arabic.

Miss Watkins, of the well-known Windswift Salukis, based her kennel on the beautiful Sabbah the Windswift. He was bred in the capital of Saudi Arabia by HH The Amir Mohammed Ibn Saud. Sabbah was presented to the Saudi Arabian Ambassador at the Court of St James's but he did not enjoy life in London and went to live with Miss Watkins who, at that time, resided in Kent. There he was mated to Windswift Yasmin and so founded the Windswift kennel.

Mr and Mrs Heard of Bridport imported a dog and a bitch from Kuwait in 1962. When they were released from quarantine they produced a litter and Mrs Heard retained two of the puppies, Taufaan Sharqi, a male, and Lateefah Sharqi, a female. The parents of these have since died — both were obtained from HH Sheik Sabah al Nasir of Kuwait. Sabah al Kuwait was a dog from a previous litter, bred identically by the Heards while they were still in Kuwait. He was brought to this country before eventually going to Libya. In England he was used by several of the large kennels, including Mrs Powell's, who breeds the Hawira Salukis, and Mrs June Williams's. The latter bred a successful litter by him out of her smooth bitch, Kumasi Khatun.

Several of the sheiks have reciprocated by importing Salukis from Britain — indeed a compliment to our breeders. These animals, for example, have been sent from the kennels of Mr Terence Thorn, Mrs Eileen Skelton-Fortune, Miss Penny Batty and Miss Mary Long. Exchanges may be infrequent, but they are two-way and American breeders have been involved also.

One comparatively recent arrival in this country is a dog, Jen Araby Mahal Bey of Sedeki, bred in America by Miss Cynthia Wood and brought here by Mr Donald Wieden of Tring in Hertfordshire. He started his show career in England in June 1973.

Like other sighthounds, the Saluki is used in Britain for sporting purposes as well as for the show ring. Saluki coursing has been practised since 1925 when it was organised, as previously mentioned, by Brigadier and Mrs Lance, and it continues to be supported enthusiastically today. It was started again in the 1950s in Scotland, where it was combined with Deerhound coursing.

At the time of writing, meetings are held in Norfolk, Yorkshire, Salisbury Plain, Northants., the Cotswolds, Lincolnshire, Hertfordshire and Scotland. Mrs Hope Waters, in her book, gives the following description of coursing in Scotland:

Coursing was re-started in 1955 and has now become an annual three-day meeting coursing blue-mountain hares on the moors outside Inverness, in which Deerhound members join, running their own stakes. Contrary to what is often supposed, on the mountain terrain these hares will give hounds some very long and spectacular courses. Also, unlike the brown hare, they go to ground. The three-day Scottish meeting has continued as an annual event since '55 and is a thoroughly social occasion with a dinner attended by all participants and to which the landowners and factors are invited. This meeting is as much a test of endurance for the owners as it is for the hounds, for the coursing is over boulder, bog, and heather on steep hillsides and wide stretches of erstwhile forest riven in places by water courses. It is ground over which no Greyhound would ever be coursed.

Mrs Waters owns one of the leading show kennels in Britain, and her famous Burydown Salukis course regularly. She was one of the Saluki Club members responsible for the recommencement of coursing in 1955. Other show prefixes to be found frequently on the coursing field are Knightellington — Mrs Helen Baker's of Headley, near Newbury — and the Almanza prefix belonging to Mr E. Tebbs whose dog, Ch. Almanza Kafiat, won the Sandpiper Trophy for the 1970/1 season and has several best-in-show wins at championship level to his credit. The Sandpiper Trophy was presented to the Saluki Club by Miss Penny Batty for the hound that has won or has been runner-up in a major coursing stake and has the most points won at championship shows during the year. Originally the coursing was organised by the Northern Coursing Club, but it is now run by a sub-committee of the Saluki Club. Until 1973 this was headed by John Boutflower, BSc, MRCVS, who had the following to say on Saluki coursing in *A Review of Coursing* by Owen Stable, *QC*, and R. M. Studdard:

> The Saluki Coursing Club differs materially from Greyhound Clubs in that our Club is an off-shoot of the Saluki or Gazelle Hound Club which is a breed society. The great advantage that the Coursing Section offers is that it ensures that there is always a proportion of the breed that not only wins in the show ring, but is capable of performing its natural function. This is not so in many breeds where frequently the show animals differ widely from their sporting counterparts (e.g. the show Greyhound). Many of our top coursing hounds win regularly on the show bench. It also has the advantage of weeding out possible hereditary defects that would not show unless subjected to the rigours of the coursing field. The Saluki is one of the half-dozen breeds that does not suffer from any of the hereditary diseases. As a practising veterinarian I feel that this is a most noteworthy point and one that is rarely considered.

Approximately ten coursing meetings are held a year with two or three stakes on the card each time. According to the book by Ann Birrell and Hope Waters on British Saluki champions, white Salukis have always been successful in the coursing field. To lend weight to this claim they give several examples, such as the pre-war coursing dogs, Haredam Viking and his daughter Knightellington Haredam Calliope — both won the Cleve Coursing Cup three times over. They were bred by Commander Adams. They cite more recent examples in Burydown Saladina, her daughters Burydown Asphodel and Freyha, and Mrs Baker's Knightellington Esmail, among others.

Two years ago Mrs Ormsby organised Saluki racing to help the Saluki Rescue Fund which is run by the breed club. Now every summer she holds Sunday racing at monthly intervals at Blindley Heath in Surrey, where Afghan racing also takes place. Usually the Salukis race over 440 yards, but Mrs Ormsby now feels that it is inadvisable to continue, as it is an unsuitable sport for the breed. She points out that the Saluki is essentially a stayer and he finds a short distance very frustrating. Animals which are normally docile become aggressive when they reach the finishing post because their speed and interest are still at a maximum.

The Saluki has had more than his share of major wins in the show ring. At the Peterborough Championship Show in 1973 Mr D. Wieden's silver dog, Ch. Sedeki Barre, was best in show — the first time a Saluki has won this award since the 1920s. However, there have been other most impressive wins. Mrs Water's Ch. Buydown Freyha was best bitch in show at Cruft's in 1964 at the age of nearly nine. She was both the winner of a major coursing stake and also the veteran stake at the height of her show career. She was also best in show at the Hound Association Championship Show, as was Miss Deborah Steed's Ch. Bedouin Caliph — he won twenty-seven challenge certificates during his career. This beautiful cream dog was bred by Mrs Lucas and Mrs James of Hedge End, near Southampton. He won his twenty-seventh ticket at the Paignton Championship Show in 1973 at the age of eight. Mrs Skelton-Fortune's Ch. Skybelle of Daxlore was the top Saluki for 1971 and 1972. She has twenty-seven challenge certificates too, was top hound, all breeds, in 1971 and has twice been best bitch, all breeds, at championship shows. She is owner-bred and comes from a particularly illustrious litter, which also included Finnish Ch. Sky Nymph of Daxlore, Swedish Ch. Skylark of Daxlore and English Ch. Sky Rocket of Daxlore. Another famous kennel is owned by Mr Terence Thorn of the Tahawi prefix. He has eight champions on his premises.

Because of breed origins the Saluki Club now holds its championship show in conjunction with the Arab Horse Society Show. Strangely enough, and luckily for the breed, the Saluki is not immensely popular in this country, but the fact that British-bred dogs are sought after in the Saluki's countries of origin is indicative of the care and research that goes into the thoughtful and selective breeding in Britain. Salukis are a credit to their owners in Britain, in Europe and in America. Part of the success must stem from the willingness and determination of British breeders to judiciously preserve and use Eastern bloodlines when they are available, so that the original breed type is never lost.

To the Arabs, the Saluki is not simply a dog. It is regarded as a spiritual hunting symbol and its beautiful streamlined appearance and fantastic working capabilities merit its reputation in the Middle East and elsewhere. From the days of the great Islamic hunter, Yazid II (*AD* 700), who allotted a slave to each of his many Salukis, they have been treated with great respect. In those times the Saluki was carried to the hunting ground on a litter. Even today, he is occasionally taken to the chase on the back of an Arab horse in acknowledgement of his dignity.

The secretary of the Saluki or Gazelle Hound Club is: Mrs J. McLeish, Grove House, 4 Watton Road, Knebworth, Herts.

THE SALUKI STANDARD

Head
Long and narrow, skull moderately wide between ears, not domed, stop not pronounced, the whole showing great quality. Nose, black or liver.

Ears
Long, and covered with long, silky hair hanging close to the skull, and mobile.

Eyes
Dark to hazel and bright, large and oval, but not prominent.

Teeth
Strong and level.

Neck
Long, supple and well muscled.

Chest
Deep and moderately narrow.

Forequarters
Shoulders sloping and set well back, well muscled without being coarse.

Forelegs
Straight and long from the elbow to the knee.

Hindquarters
Strong, hip-bones set wide apart, and stifle moderately bent, hocks low to the ground, showing galloping and jumping power.

Loins and back
Back fairly broad, muscles slightly arched over the loin.

Feet
Of moderate length, toes long and well arched, not splayed out, but at the same time not cat-footed, the whole being strong and supple and well feathered between the toes.

Tail
Long, set on low, and carried naturally in a curve, well feathered on the underside with long, silky hair, not bushy.

Coat
Smooth and of a soft, silky texture, slight feather on the legs, feather at the back of the thighs, and sometimes with a slight woolly feather on thighs and shoulders.

Colours
White, cream, fawn, golden, red, grizzle and tan, tricolour (black, white and tan) and black and tan.

General appearance
The whole appearance of this breed should give an impression of grace and symmetry, and of great speed and endurance, coupled with strength and activity to enable it to kill gazelle or other quarry over deep sand or rocky mountain. The expression should be dignified and gentle, with deep, faithful, far-seeing eyes. Dogs should be average in height from 23-28in.; bitches may be considerably smaller, this being very typical of the breed.

14

The Whippet

The Whippet is the most adaptable of all the Gazehound breeds in that it is perfectly suited to compete at a show one day, a race meeting the next and a coursing event on the third day. A good dog can be in the prizes for all three on account of the breed's remarkable versatility. Furthermore, because coursing and racing are fundamentally amateur, the dogs are owner-trained and do not develop the exaggerated muscling that one sees on working Greyhounds. Whippets are also excellent ratters and will even point game. Despite their fine skin, they will go through thick cover to flush rabbits.

The origins of the breed are nearly always said to be Terrier crossed with either Greyhound or Italian Greyhound. The Terrier may have been anything from a Manchester or Bedlington to a Staffordshire. A number of writers give the opinion that Whippets originated specifically in the North of England. Many breed members, however, subscribe to neither of these views. Greyhounds and Terriers are constantly crossed in the Northern Counties of England to this day, and the resulting litters are declared to be Whippets, despite the fact that they bear little resemblance to them.

One has only to see the thirteenth-century hound with the Berger du Jube at Chartres Cathedral, the white dog in the January series of the fifteenth-century manuscript *Les Tres Riches Heures du Duc de Berry* at the Musée Condé at Chantilly, or the pale hound in the sixteenth-century French tapestry *La Dame à la Licorne*, at the Cluny Museum in Paris, to know exactly where the Whippet originated.

There have been various types of hounds for centuries and all differ in height. Presumably the Whippet has developed from the smooth-coated, small variety, as has the Italian Greyhound. I can do no better than quote from Mr C. H.

135

Douglas Todd's book *The Popular Whippet,* in which he says:

> To sum up this very interesting subject, which I am certain can be one of surmise only, it seems that a Whippet is a small dog of Greyhound-type of great antiquity. That, from what the ancient artists show us, a dog similar to a Whippet has been a favourite model for their various types of artistic creations; sculpture over the centuries, pottery and so on. That he is closely akin to the Greyhound and Italian Greyhound and that there is no evidence to prove him otherwise.

Although it would seem that the Whippet did not originate in the North of England, the Northerners must be given credit for being the first to realise the Whippet's potential, both as a rabbit catcher and a racer after the rag. The latter sport is still practised on Sunday mornings in that part of the world. The dogs are hand-slipped down the course to their owner, who waves a rag and shouts encouragement. When the dog reaches the end of the track, he jumps to catch the rag, which he has been taught to tear and run to since he was a puppy. There is great art in hand-slipping. The dog is held by the scruff of the neck and by the tail. He is then literally thrown down the course and by this method can gain on his opponents. Racing elsewhere in the country is very different. Whippets run from electrically worked traps to a dummy hare and over distances ranging from 150 to 260 yards. The shorter race is on the straight, the longer distance is run on an oval track with two bends. Further details of racing are given in an earlier chapter.

The top racing sire at present is Miss Barbara Rooney's Russettwood Pageant, now aged ten. He has produced five racing champions to date. He is by Mrs McKay's famous Ch. Laguna Ligonier, himself father of numerous show, track and coursing winners, as is the same owner's Ch. Laguna Light Lagoon. Another successful racing sire, the late Shalfleet Saga, was owned by the writer and Mrs Caroline Brown. He produced two racing champions and is sire and grandsire of ten WCRA finalists and other racing winners.

He was bred by Mrs Wilton-Clark. All these dogs come from show stock, so the breed can hardly be said to be split.

Show kennels also contribute substantially to a number of coursing winners. The Whippet Coursing Club is the parent body and was founded in 1963. It has approximately fifty members. Whippets adapt well to coursing and are able to tackle a hare. About a dozen meetings are held a year by the National Whippet Coursing Club. This organisation has ground in the Oxfordshire, Huntingdonshire and Hertfordshire areas. In the last two years three more clubs have been formed, the East Anglian Whippet Coursing Club, the East of England WCC, which plans to course in Sussex and as far north as the Wash, and the Woolley WCC in Huntingdonshire. Each club limits its membership so that all dogs obtain a nomination during the season.

Available land is so limited that, with an over-subscribed club, some members' dogs would not otherwise get a course. When the parent body was formed only about seven of the show kennels coursed, now there are nine and most course the dogs they show. Furthermore, numbers of the top coursing Whippets over the last ten years have again been produced by the show kennels, and outstanding dogs have tended to come once again from the Laguna, Dragonhill, Allways, Tweseldown or Nimrodel bloodlines.

As with Greyhounds, classes are provided at most breed-club shows for dogs that have been raced or coursed. The Whippet Club also stipulates that each dog entered must have won a race, or course. The winners of the racing or coursing trophies over the last few years have all been dogs which have won well in the show ring as well as in the field. At the Whippet Club Open Show in October 1973, for example, the winner of best in show, and the racing/coursing cup was Lady Anderson's Ch. Tweseldown Winchat. There are many other show winners running under Racing Association or Coursing Club rules. These include Mrs Lowe's Ch. Nimrodel Willow Daughter and Ch. Nimrodel Ruff, Mrs McKay's Laguna Lennox, Mrs Meek's Whippet Club racing champion Chancerick Koh-i-Noor, and Chancerick Nimrodel Rosefinch, Miss Rooney's Russettwood Enchanted and many more.

Whippets have increased immensely in popularity in this country over the last ten years, and are no longer frowned on as miners' dogs. Indeed, their registration figures at the Kennel Club now stand second to those of the Afghan. Like the Irish Wolfhound they are, unfortunately, finding their way into the hands of dealers and puppy factories. Their multiple uses make them obvious pets and now that coursing and racing have such support it is unlikely that their numbers will decrease. A rescue service is provided for this breed, as for the other Gazehounds, and about forty dogs are rescued and placed in new homes each year.

With the increase in numbers has come a corresponding increase in stature, particularly in the show ring, although the Kennel Club standard gives the ideal heights of a dog and a bitch as 18½in. and 17½in. respectively, there is little doubt that a number of top show bitches measure more than 19in. and some of the dogs more than 20in. Size is an extremely inflammatory subject within the breed and few can agree on it, so the final answer must rest with the judges. What is most important is that an extremely high standard has been reached, and bitch classes particularly often contain as many as thirty really beautiful specimens. The Whippet, as the smallest Gazehound in Britain, should be portable and therefore small enough for the poacher to carry under his coat if necessary. There are still some small ones being bred, however, and there is no doubt that they are quicker on the turn, although the larger hounds may be faster on the straight.

Probably the most famous small dog champion was Mrs Cooke's (at that time Mrs Jones) Ch. Fieldspring Bartsia of Allways. He sired countless winning puppies and five champions. He gained his title in 1953, as did his litter sister, Ch. Fieldspring Betony, and he is behind the majority of modern pedigrees. Mr Douglas Todd's Ch. Wingedfoot Marksman Allways was another famous and successful dog and sired ten show champions, as did Ch. Pilot Officer Prune owned by Mrs Chapman. The breed record is held by Mrs McKay's Ch. Laguna Ligonier, sire of twelve champions.

The record for the most challenge certificates won in

the show ring is held by Mrs Knight's Ch. Dondelayo Roulette with twenty. The runner-up is Mrs Argyle's Ch. Harque the Lark with one fewer. Her kennel has produced many successful champions, most of which go back to their bitch, Wingedfoot Tu Whit Tu Whoo, and the dog, Ch. Runway Controller, bred by Mrs Argyle.

Another champion that will always be remembered is Mr and Mrs H. Wood's beautiful particolour bitch, Ch. Laguna Ravensdowne Astri, winner of eleven certificates during 1966 and 1967, and Mr Boundy's fawn dog, Ch. Sticklepath Saracen. He won nine, the last of these being awarded at Paignton Championship Show in 1973 when he was seven. The Whippet to achieve the highest honour ever at Cruft's was Mrs Knight's Ch. Dondelayo Duette, reserve best in show all breeds to the Bull Terrier, Ch. Abraxas Audacity, in 1972. Another dog, Mr F. Jones's famous Ch. Robmaywin Stargazer of Allways, won the Hound group there in 1958, and in 1975 the group was won by Mrs Wright's Beseeka Knight Errant of Silkstone.

It would be impossible to single out any one kennel as there have been so many well to the fore over the last fifty years, but there are some kennels no longer existing which have had such a tremendous influence on the breed and on modern dogs that they must be mentioned: Mrs Cooke's Allways kennel, Mr Douglas Todd's Wingedfoot Whippets and Mrs Lewis's 'of Test' prefix are behind countless dogs winning today, in particular Mrs Wilton-Clark's Shalfleet kennel which was started with a bitch called Wingedfoot Bartette, bred by Mr Douglas Todd. The Shalfleets have produced ten whippet champions.

Mrs Wigg, of the famous Ladiesfield prefix, unfortunately died at the beginning of 1973, but the kennel's bloodlines were continued by her daughter, Miss Penny Batty. The Dragonhill kennel closed down when its owner, Mrs Cleeve, died in 1966, but Mrs Ian Lowe, of Kingham, Oxon, has much of her stock and has based her Nimrodel kennel on Dragonhill breeding.

In this breed, more than any other Gazehound variety, there has been a concentrated effort to increase the quality of the coloured hounds such as blacks and blues. An extremely high standard has now been realised in these colours, progress entirely the result of the dedication and interest of Mrs Poppy Martin, who has been breeding Whippets since 1911, and Mrs Margaret Wigg. Mrs Martin bred one of the only two black female champions with Poppy Black Tarquin. The other belonged to Mrs K. Barnsley and Mrs D. Whitwell. From Mrs Wigg's kennel came the only black male champion, Ladiesfield Starturn. Both breeders spent much time and energy tracing the bloodlines and history of the coloured dogs through many generations.

The Whippet seems in no danger of becoming less versatile, but he could lose his type and most endearing characteristics if the breed becomes too commercialised. At the time of writing, this seems a distinct possibility. Too many owners are breeding haphazardly and a number of discarded Whippets need homes. These are highly sensitive, intelligent hounds, and the rapid increase in registrations could lead to disaster. On the other hand, there are more beautiful Whippets being bred and shown currently than ever before, and British bloodlines are undoubtedly the best anywhere in the world.

The names and address of breed club secretaries are as follows:

The East Anglian Whippet Club
Mrs V. Webb, Padneyhill Farm, Wicken, Ely, Cambs.

The Midland Whippet Club
Mr A. Raines, Wick Lodge, Manor Road, Wick, Nr Bristol.

The National Whippet Association
Mrs Rawlings, Chyton, Fielden Lane, Crowborough, Sussex.

The Northern Counties Whippet Club
Mrs J. Rollason, 86 Station Road, Blackpool, FY4 1HB.

The Northern Ireland Whippet Club
Miss M. Sloan, 24 Seymour Street, Lisburn, Co. Antrim.

The Whippet Club
Mrs D. McKay, Laguna Kennel, Brightwalton, Nr Newbury, Berks.

The Whippet Club of Scotland
Mrs Buglass, 12 Queensferry Road, Kirk, West Lothian.

The Whippet Club of Wales
Mr B. Morgan, 25 Manor Park, Brynn Road, Pencoed, Nr Bridgend, Glam.

THE WHIPPET STANDARD

General appearance
Should convey an impression of beautifully balanced muscular power and strength, combined with great elegance and grace of outline. Symmetry of outline, muscular development and powerful gait are the main considerations; the dog, being built for speed and work, all forms of exaggeration should be avoided. The dog should possess great freedom of action, the forelegs should be thrown forward and low over the ground like a thoroughbred horse, not in a hackney-like action. Hindlegs should come well under the body, giving great propelling power, general movement not to look stilted, high-stepping or short and mincing in manner.

Head and skull
Long and lean, flat on top tapering to the muzzle, rather wide between the eyes, the jaws powerful and clean-cut; Nose black, in blues a bluish colour is permitted and in livers a nose of the same colour. In whites or particolours a butterfly nose is permissible.

Eyes
Bright, expression very alert.

Ears
Rose-shaped, small and fine in texture.

Mouth
Level. The teeth in the top jaw fitting closely over the teeth in the lower jaw.

Neck
Long and muscular, elegantly arched.

Forequarters
Shoulders oblique and muscular with the blades carried up to the spine, closely set together at the top. Forelegs straight and upright, front not too wide, pasterns strong with slight spring, elbows well set under the body.

Body
Chest very deep and plenty of heart room, brisket deep and well defined; back broad, firm, somewhat long and showing a definite arch over the loin, but not humped, loin giving the impression of strength and power; ribs well sprung; well muscled on back.

Hindquarters
Strong and broad across the thighs, stifles well bent, hocks well let down, second thighs strong, the dog then being able to stand over a lot of ground and show great driving power.

Feet
Very neat, well split up between the toes, knuckles highly arched, pads thick and strong.

Tail
No feathering. Long, tapering, when in action carried in a delicate curve upwards, but not over the back.

Coat
Fine, short, as close as possible in texture.

Colour
Any colour or mixture of colours.

Size
The ideal height for dogs is 18½in. and for bitches 17½in. Judges should use discretion and not unduly penalise an otherwise good specimen.

FAULTS

Front and shoulders
Weak, sloping or too straight pasterns, pigeon toes, tied elbows, loaded or bossy shoulders wide on top and straight shoulder blades, flat sides. An exaggerated narrow front not to be encouraged.

Head and skull
Apple skull, short foreface or downface.

Ears
Pricked or tulip.

Mouth
Overshot or undershot.

Neck
Throatiness at join of neck and jaw, and at base of neck.

Body and hindquarters
A short-coupled or cramped stance, an exaggerated arch, a camel or humped back (with arch starting behind shoulder blades), too short or over long loins. Straight stifles, poor muscular development of thighs and second thighs.

Feet
Splayed, flat or open.

Tail
Gay, ringed or twisted, short or docked.

Coat
Wire- or broken-coated, a coarse or woolly coat, coarse thick skin.

15

The Gazehound in North America and Europe

The Gazehound's activities both in America and Europe are as varied as they are in this country. Although coursing is rarely practised in Europe, racing is very highly organised and competitive. A very full racing calendar, covering events throughout Europe, is published at the beginning of the season.

Coursing is practised in America where, until recently, it was called hunting. All Gazehounds compete in this sport. Rules have been drawn up and compiled by a body of Gazehound enthusiasts with a representative for each breed. The system of coursing is different from the British one. Three or four hounds are slipped together, having been drawn in order at the start of the meeting. The dogs are with owners or handlers and there is no slipper. When the hunt master gives the word, the owners slip the hounds. Two judges are present and the dog's performance is judged in much the same way as under the British system.

The comparatively new sport of lure coursing with a dummy is also practised in America over a distance of 375, 440 or, occasionally, 880 yards. The lure is pulled by an electric motor similar to that used for racing. Points are given for eagerness, endurance, agility and recall to the owners. Hounds are timed over the first 100 yards and points are also given for speed. Afghans, Salukis, Borzois and Whippets enjoy it enormously, as do Greyhounds, which are outstandingly successful at it. Wolfhounds and Deerhounds are not very interested in coursing a dummy.

Greyhound racing came to America before its success in Britain. In the US dogs run on sand instead of grass. All racing is organised by the National Greyhound Racing

Commission, and all racing litters are registered with the National Coursing Association. On most tracks there are eight runners — two more than in Britain — and some even run as many as nine dogs at a time. The distances of the races vary from 300 yards to just over 600 yards. As in Britain, the sport is a professional one; likewise in Australia, where the tracks are quite exceptional. Harold Park, Sydney, is said to be one of the best in the world, is grass and 642 yards in circumference.

Another Gazehound that races in America and Canada is the Whippet. It runs over 200 yard tracks on a highly organised, but amateur, basis. The American and Canadian dogs compete against each other several times a year. There, as is the occasional custom on the Continent, the dogs are put in open metal cages between races to prevent them from tearing the upholstery of their owners' cars in their excitement and anxiety to reach the lure.

British breeding has done much for the American show scene. American Afghan breeders imported a dog, Ch. Badshah of Ainsdart, when first founding their stock. Although he himself does not appear to have been exceptional, many of his grandchildren and great-grandchildren were quite outstanding. The only Afghan to be best in show at Westminster was Ch. Shirkan of Grandeur, who is behind many of today's show winners.

One of the greatest American Borzois must be the top winner for 1971 and 1972 — American and Canadian champion Sirhan Poraschai. He was bred in Canada by Mr and Mrs Benbow of the Sirhan kennels and his owners, Ed Abbott and George Root, live in California. He has several best-in-show wins and numerous awards. He was one of the top ten hounds for 1971 and 1972, and is a most handsome, almost all-white dog with a few black markings.

In Deerhounds, Mr and Mrs Pilat, Mrs Gerber, Mrs Lewis and Mrs Arnold all own successful hounds. On a visit to Britain in 1971 Mr and Mrs Pilat toured some of the top Deerhound kennels and returned to America with a young dog, Reilly of Enterkine, bred by Miss Bell.

A Greyhound import that was top bitch in 1970 was Ch.

Shalfleet Spanish Moon, bred by Frank Brown and owned in England by Mrs Barbara Wilton-Clark. She achieved this record in only 4½ months of showing. Another beautiful bitch from the same kennel was English and American Champion Shalfleet Starlight of Foxden.

In Greyhounds, every American show dog seems to have originated from Mrs de Casembroot's Ch. Treetops Hawk. He sired thirty champions and he himself won sixteen challenge certificates. Among his progeny is English and American Champion Seagift Parcancady Royaltan. He himself sired eleven champions and has twenty-one champion grand-children.

As American breeding, in the Misses Harrison and Atfield's Ch. Rory of Kihone and American Champion Cragwood Barney O'Shea of Riverlawn, has done much for British Wolfhounds, so the reverse has happened in America. One influential dog by Mrs Nagle's famous Ch. Sulhamstead Concara (mentioned in Chapter 10 on the breed) was Sulhamstead Dan of Ambleside. Another of the first imports to improve the breed was Felixstowe Kilmorac. There is, therefore, much common blood between British and American Wolfhounds. Two recent successful exports from England to America are Canadian and American Ch. Sulhamstead Malice, which is out of the famous brood bitch, Ch. Sulhamstead Modena, and Ch. Petasmeade Fiana, sired by the highly successful Ch. Caio of Eaglescrag.

A great supporter of the Pharaoh Hound is Mrs Rita Laventhall-Sacks who established the Pharaoh Hound Club of America and a registry for all hounds imported to and bred in America. So far 250 hounds are registered. Mrs Sacks bred the first international champion in Beltara's Amun-Re, a dog that was exported to Mexico with a bitch from her kennel, Beltara's Neferu.

The general type and high quality of the American Salukis can be credited to Mr Edward Aldrich of Rhode Island, who imported dogs from the Sarona and Amherstia kennels in the 1930s to found his own stock. From these, many of the modern dogs trace their origins.

British-bred Whippets have done extremely well in the

American show ring. One of the most outstanding Gazehounds to be exported was the Whippet, Ch. Courtenay
Fleetfoot, a particolour dog bred in England by Mr Halliwell.
He won twenty-eight Hound groups and was best in show all
breeds, not only at the Westminster Show — the US
equivalent of Cruft's — but at the Chicago, Harrisburg and
Harbor City shows as well. Several other British-bred Whippets
have made names for themselves in the USA. Just a few of
these are the International Champion Laguna Leisure, who
gained his title in Britain, America and Canada and was bred
by Mrs McKay near Newbury, Berks., Ch. Selbrook Highlight,
bred by Mrs Selby and Ch. Greenbrae Barn Dance, bred by
Mrs Yerburgh.

EUROPE

Showing and racing on the Continent are run in most
countries by the Union Internationale des Clubs de Lévriers.
The majority of European countries, including Sweden,
Finland and Czechoslovakia, are members. The most notable
exceptions are Portugal and Luxembourg. No coursing is
available through the UICL and the only countries to practise
Greyhound coursing are Spain and Portugal. The latter
organises a great coursing event each year, which is similar to
the Waterloo Cup. In Spain professional Greyhound racing is
very popular and there are approximately six major tracks in
operation. All other countries in Europe race on a strictly
amateur basis.

Each country represented in the UICL has three secretaries,
one for racing, another for showing and a third for general
matters. The most coveted award of the year is the Schöneit
und Rennleistung plaque for the dog that has been most
successful in the show ring and on the race track.

The UICL run race meetings throughout the year in
various countries. However, there are two major events held
each autumn: the UICL European Championship, for the
best racing dogs of the preceding year from each country,
and the UICL Titelrennen Championship, an open event.

Both championships are held in one of five countries — Switzerland, Holland, Austria, Germany or Hungary. The larger hounds run over 475 metres or 518 yards and the Whippets over 350 metres or 382 yards. The lure is returned on a go-cart between each race, an extremely quick method. The Dutch stadium in Amsterdam is one of the best in Europe, has a covered stand for the spectators and a range of specially designed kennels built behind the stadium buildings out of sight of the track, so that the dogs should not become over-excited between races.

Each finalist receives a prize of an embroidered coat, and on it in gold letters is the name of the championship and the year it was won. Bouquets are also presented to the first four dogs in each final. All winning dogs are given their prizes on a podium and then parade down the track to music. Afghans, Borzois, Greyhounds, Salukis and Whippets all compete in these events.

The show system on the Continent is slightly different from the British. All dogs in Europe are graded in three sections: *bon, très bon* and *excellent*. The judge writes a report on each and this is published later in the breed magazine. The CAC, an award similar to our challenge certificate, is presented to the best dog and bitch. If the show is an international one, there is a CACIB on offer as well to the best of the winning dogs. Champions may not compete for the CAC, only for the CACIB. These rules apply to any country that is a member of the Fédération Cynologique Internationale, and this includes Scandinavia.

One of the most successful Gazehounds in Sweden is Bo Bengtson's Greyhound, Black and White Lady. She not only gained her title in Sweden and Norway, but was brought to England in 1972 and won a CC at her first show the day after she came out of quarantine. After becoming an English champion she was returned to Sweden. Her owner also has a number of successful show Whippets, some of which were bred in England. These include the international Ch. Laguna **Leader, Badgewood Mark Twain** and **English** and Scandinavian Ch. Fleeting Flamboyant.

Another famous Scandinavian Gazehound champion is

Miss Carin Lindhe's English-bred International Champion, Asphodel Arabis. Miss Lindhe also owns a top winning Irish Wolfhound, Swedish Champion Mountebanks Barrabas, who was owner-bred out of a British bitch. A Deerhound from the same kennel, Ch. Mountebanks Nadis is also highly successful and is by a British-bred Ardkinglas sire. Other champion Salukis in that part of the world are the Finnish Sky Nymph of Daxlore and the Swedish Skylark of Daxlore, mentioned in an earlier chapter.

Dr Quaritsch in West Germany has the Deerhound Ardkinglas New Dawn who has twenty-eight CACIBs and is an international and national champion of Germany, France, Monaco, Switzerland, Austria, Hungary and Luxembourg.

In the other parts of Europe it is not so easy to pick out individual dogs for mention. Most Dutch Whippets originate from British stock in Wingedfoot Jacky Lantern and Blue Moon. Another British dog, Vahlay Golden Gander, bred by Mrs Weir, is to be found in most Dutch pedigrees.

One of the most successful breeders of Salukis and Whippets in Holland is Mr Tim Teiller of the Samoems prefix, whose cream Whippets are so much alike that it is almost impossible to tell them apart. Mrs Hugenholtz, secretary of the Dutch Whippet Club, owned and bred Caspar of the Thunder Rangers, a winner of the coveted Schönheit und Rennleistung award. A well-known Afghan breeder from that country is Mrs Eva Pauptit of the van de Oranje Manege kennels, who has exported hounds all over the world. Although she breeds very few Afghans now, most of the Dutch stock originates from her bloodlines.

In France one does not see as many British imports among the Gazehounds. Many of the Greyhounds are Belgian-bred, but the classes are poorly filled. The Borzois and Salukis too are mostly bred on the Continent. Whippets, however, have been imported to France with considerable success. The Tinribs kennel was founded by an Englishwoman, Mrs Stancomb, who was at one time domiciled in France, and her stock has had great influence on the modern Whippet. French champion Tinribs Tinkerblue was extremely successful as was her black bitch, Tinribs Twinrivers Nightshade. To become a French champion it is necessary to win the CACIB at the big Paris Show held in March. No matter how many CAC or CACIB awards a dog has won, only Paris can make it a champion. In the last five years the bitch CACIB has been won three times by British-bred animals: in 1970 by the Comtesse de Saint-Seine's French champion Laguna Leonora, a brindle and white bred by Mrs McKay; and in 1971 and 1972 by the Comtesse de Béarn's French champion Martinsell Piquet, bred by the writer and Mrs Caroline Brown.

In Portugal there is a thriving Afghan and Saluki kennel owned by Miss Carla Molinari, who lives at Estoril. Her Saluki, International Ch. Burydown Ziska, bred by Mrs Hope Waters, had, at the last count, nine CAC and eight CACIB awards, won in Portugal, Spain, France, Italy and Monte Carlo. She also owns another British-bred Saluki, Ch. Burydown Wahshad, and a Swedish-bred one, Ch. Mountebanks Darius. In Afghans, Miss Molinari's Ch. Musqat do Vale Negro has seven CAC and CACIBs and her brother, Mandrake, has two CAC awards won in Portugal, and a CACIB won in Spain.

Italy's Mrs Kukavici has imported Whippets from the Glenbervie Courthill and Dondelayo kennels and is building on this stock to found her own breeding. Frau Frankenberger in Germany has a thriving kennel of Afghans, which includes International Champion Gilosi el Jaira that was the top winning Afghan in Europe in 1972. She has produced six international champions in Germany, Czechoslovakia, Italy and Hungary.

One of the most successful racing and show Whippets in Austria was Spirit of Greyish Blue Sweeper, another winner of the Schönheit und Rennleistung award and sire of a number of other race winners in Europe. In Switzerland, Mr Carlo Weber, a UICL representative, has a competitive kennel of Greyhounds and Whippets.

The success of British-bred dogs has been deliberately accentuated in this chapter because this is a book on British bloodlines and general progress in the Gazehound breeds, so our exports should be of interest. There are many foreign breeders producing excellent stock without having introduced

British blood. Nevertheless, in many countries British dogs have influenced the Gazehound breeds considerably.

It is therefore regrettable that there are still many sub-standard animals leaving this country. It is, of course, gross dishonesty to export an animal that is not entire, has a bad mouth, the wrong number of teeth or incorrect ear carriage. Unfortunately, this happens all too often. If we want a good name for dogs abroad — and only the winners are mentioned in this book — we must be more particular about the dogs we export. If the buyer wishes to pay a small amount for a puppy of only 12 - 15 weeks old then he must realise that he is taking a risk that the animal will not mature as he hopes. If, on the other hand, a nearly adult dog is being sent abroad unseen, it is the vendor's responsibility to see that the buyer has a fair deal. Ears and teeth, in particular, are all important on the Continent and most British breeders are aware of this, but, even so, too many indifferent dogs are sent abroad and spoil our reputation.

Epilogue

This is not a textbook because it does not include many of the details with which academics are concerned. The purpose was to describe and discuss the wider aspects of the group of dogs known as Gazehounds — those that hunt by sight rather than scent.

To avoid all detail is to endanger truth as a result of excessive generalisation. But there is a vast library of books and publications, good and indifferent, written by life-long devotees of the dog on the subject of their respective breeds. It is these works, and not this book, that enthusiasts in search of information on the breeding, rearing and showing of specific dogs should consult. This, however, is the first work in English on the Gazehounds as a character group.

The intention has been to give prominence to the effect of geography on the Gazehound and to destroy several illusions about their origins of some of the breeds. At this juncture a clash of opinions must arise. The views expressed here, whilst certainly the responsibility of the author, are the result of painstaking research by other experts and represent a collation of the best opinion.

Nevertheless, it is not only possible but inevitable that particular owners will resent the discarding of a number of long and fiercely held beliefs, and perhaps a few household gods may suffer. If this promotes discussion among enthusiasts, so much the better. It need not cause acrimony. In the words of Somerset Maughan, 'He who knows something for certain has ceased to think.'

In the future of Gazehounds there are various present faults of construction which, if exaggerated, could detract from the appearance and working capabilities of each breed. Size is the most discussed and arguable question of all. It has contributed to the split in many of the Gundog breeds and was instrumental in the division between the various types of

Greyhound. The Gundog, in the case of the Setter for example, has become too leggy and tall and, in the Retriever breeds, too stocky and heavy. The show Greyhound is normally taller and finer than his racing or coursing cousins.

Increase or decrease in height does not involve all Gazehound breeds, but Wolfhounds and Whippets have undoubtedly become taller over the last ten years. The former tend to lose bulk and become, as described by one breeder, a silhouette dog, without the powerful chest and necessary width in front, so that there would be difficulty in tackling a large and aggressive quarry. Exaggerated length of leg too tends to slow the turning ability of any dog and Saluki coursing enthusiasts frequently claim that the best workers seem to be lower on the ground.

Whippets in America are several inches taller than those in Britain and, in consequence, are finer all through, with a tendency to slab sides. Another feature of the fine hound is flat, extra-long shoulder blades. If this becomes exaggerated, the blades will almost meet near the spine, so that, as the dog bends down to kill, the tips of the blades touch and he is unable to reach out and down.

Conversely, if bred down in size the Gazehound can lose length of neck, loin and leg, and this leads to a short-legged stuffy appearance. Strangely enough, heads also tend to suffer when size diminishes. A short head on a Gazehound is a bad fault. It must have the necessary length of muzzle and strength of jaw to grip and despatch its quarry. In some Continental countries, essentially France, Switzerland, Austria and Germany, the Gazehound breeds are smaller and definitely shorter in head. In Whippets particularly, this produces a tendency to apple skulls and bulging eyes.

The standards of the breeds were constructed with care as each became popular in this country. Size and stature were based on the first and best examples from their countries of origin — and who are we to say that our hounds are better than the first imports, when we haven't seen the modern dog work in his native surroundings? If recommended heights in the standards are ignored, then they may as well not exist. Obviously an inch either side of the standard height does not matter very much, even in the smaller Gazehound breeds, but if bigger dogs are bred to others of a similar stamp, the whole breed could be affected, as has happened in the groups already mentioned.

This problem is entirely in the hands of the judges. No one can prevent breeders from producing dogs which are too large or too small, but if they fail to win prizes in the ring the owner may be forced to reconsider his breeding programme.

The other all-important feature of any Gazehound is good eyesight. There are hounds being bred today with small, beady eyes. When watching a number of Gazehounds hunting, the ones with the large, bright eyes have the best and most dependable sight. Many owners claim that light-eyed hounds can see farther than those with dark eyes. This is doubtful, but hounds with small eyes can be seen waiting for a reaction from those with good vision before they sight the quarry for themselves. Furthermore, the eyes in all Gazehounds should be set far apart so that they can glimpse moving objects on either side of them as well as directly ahead. A hound with correctly placed eyes will not turn his head if his owner goes to left or right of him, but can watch out of the corner of each eye. The ability to scan is vital.

Another important quality is temperament. These problems are often difficult to eliminate as aggressive or nervous dispositions can occur for no apparent reason. Rearing plays an important part in the behaviour pattern of any animal. Providing puppies are handled frequently and talked to at an early age, they normally mature with friendly, outgoing temperaments, unless there is a streak of bad temper or nerves in their breeding. A certain amount of freedom is also vital and gradual introduction to the noises of machines and traffic. Nerves can of course be due to inbreeding or to combining unsuitable temperaments, but any strain that repeatedly produces excessive timidity or the reverse should be discontinued.

Gazehounds should have extrovert but trustworthy personalities. They are famous for their dependability with children. At the same time they must be fierce enough to chase when necessary. It is perhaps difficult to strike a happy medium. Aggression can result from racing and Greyhounds and Whippets will often behave uncharacteristically after a strenuous racing programme. When in a pack they may bark at or chase another dog smaller than themselves, a tendency which would not have become evident had they not been trained to watch for a lure.

Although neither temperament nor eyesight constitute serious problems at present, size will always be a worry because this factor alone can cloud the demarcation line between the breeds. The Wolfhound and Deerhound could conceivably become so alike that it would be impossible to distinguish between them. If the Whippet or the Pharaoh Hound increase in height they start to develop Greyhound characteristics. In the Whippet the topline begins to flatten, and the arch over the loin, which is so typical of the breed, is lost.

The smallest Greyhound to win the Waterloo Cup was the bitch Coomassie, who, at 42lb, was only 12lb heavier than some of the Whippets winning today. With breeds that all stemmed from a similar source there must always be a danger that they will amalgamate once more. As most breeders have the future of the Gazehound very much at heart, it is unlikely that any problem will be allowed to escalate. Unfortunately there is always the danger in the popular breeds that an establishment producing exclusively for gain will breed and sell untypical specimens which, in their turn, will give birth to unsound, wrongly constructed progeny. This must be the greatest problem now, and it is up to the genuine Gazehound owners among us to solve it.

Bibliography

The Afghan Hound by Charles Harrisson (Popular Dogs Publishing Co.)

Borzois by Winifred E. Chadwick (Kemp's Printing and Publishing Co.)

British Dogs by A. Croxton-Smith (Collins).

British Sports and Sportsmen (Sports and Sportsmen).

Coursing and Falconry by Harding Cox and the Hon. Gerald Lascelles (Longmans, Green).

The Deerhound by A. N. Hartley (East Midland Allied Press).

The Dog by Fernand Mery (Cassell).

The Dog in Sport by J. Wentworth Day (Harrap).

Dogs, Dogs, Dogs by Howard Loxton (Hamlyn).

The Dogs of the British Islands by Stonehenge (Horace Cox).

Dogs of Today by Major Harding Cox; revised by Stanley Dangerfield (Black).

The Greyhound by Edwards Clarke (Popular Dogs Publishing Co.).

Greyhound and Mechanical Lure Racing by William H. Bracht (Angus and Robertson).

The Irish Wolfhound by Father Edmund Hogan and *The Irish Wolfhound* by Captain G. A. Graham (M. H. Gill & Son, Dublin).

The Complete Irish Wolfhound by Alma Starbuck (Bowell House Inc., New York, USA).

The Irish Wolfhound by P. Gardner (Dundalgan Press, Dundalk).

The Kennel Club Stud Book

Of Pedigree Unknown by Phill Drabble (Cassell).

156

The Saluki Book of British Champions by Ann Birrell and Hope Waters.

The Saluki in History, Art and Sport by Hope and David Waters (David and Charles).

The Popular Whippet by C. H. Douglas-Todd (Popular Dogs Publishing Co.).

Whippets by E. Fitch Daglish (W. and G. Foyle).

Zehntausend und 75 Jahre Hetzhunde / Windhunde (Deutschen Windhundzucht und Rennerband).

JOURNALS

Think Afghan (Afghan Hound Association).

The Borzoi Year Book (the Borzoi Club).

Der Windhund Freund.

Dog World.

The Greyhound Club Year Book.

The Gazehound.

Harp and Hound (Irish Wolfhound Association).

The Irish Wolfhound (Irish Wolfhound Club).

The Whippet (the Whippet Club.).

Index

158